The Art and Science of Daily Business Transformation

Everyday Turnaround™

Turnaround (noun) - a positive change, improvement[1]
Turnaround (verb) - improve significantly

Eric Kish

---

[1] The Cambridge Dictionary

Contents

Introduction

The guy who hired me to do my first turnarounds was a smart guy. He'd give me, on average, 18 months to complete a turnaround and then overnight and without warning, he'd move me to the next one. I was not allowed to take any of the people I had trained and coached in previous turnarounds. I had to start from scratch with every new company.

Typically, I had little time to prepare for the next turnaround. I had to get my bearings fast and "fly the airplane while it was being built." This meant that while discovering and developing assumptions, I needed to act in a way that would persuade the organization to follow. I also knew the day would come when I would suddenly move on to my next challenge, leaving behind a leadership team and an organization that could continue to fly the plane without me. This had been my routine for 10 years, resulting in seven successful turnarounds.

Doing these turnarounds, I experimented with various tools and methods. I was strongly inspired by the Kaizen practice of continuous improvement and later by Scrum.[2] A team-based approach to project completion, it was embraced by software development

---

[2] Scrum is an Agile framework for completing complex projects.

organizations after the *Agile Manifesto* was published in 2001. In fact, this book was written and published using a Scrum ritual.

The other pillar of my approach was discovering behavioral science and the tools that allow a leader to understand inherent employee drives and needs as well as how to align them with organizational roles.

Everyday Turnaround is about turnaround tactics. It provides a pragmatic view of the challenges a leader faces and the daily rituals that can be embedded in the muscle memory of the organization. It's also about helping an organization's people figure out how to row in the same direction, having each one fit naturally to the role while delivering continuous, fact-based improvement—all synced by an organizational heartbeat.

Everyday Turnaround is the result of testing the concepts in 12 turnarounds across seven industries on three continents over 18 years. It describes a fictional organization inspired by my own experiences; any resemblance to real people or actual names is purely by chance. The story emphasizes how agility is the key to the success of a turnaround while applying the Observe-Orient-Decide-Act concept developed by the military for its combat operations processes. Its approach helps you understand how to apply the principles and tools in a non-theoretical, real-world environment.

Heading Into the Storm

Synchronicity

Mark had just wrapped up a successful turnaround when Will, his agent, called to say that Energon was looking for a turnaround CEO.

The lender had told Will that Energon was burning cash quickly and the board had recently fired the CEO. The company had no time for the typical national executive search and, frankly, it would be hard to find someone interested in joining a company in free fall. This dire situation had to be addressed—and fast—to save the company.

Energon's lender was worried the company had no business leader in place to navigate the company out of the storm battering its operations. Mark wasn't interested in a new job at the time, but Will insisted he should explore this opportunity.

Although he was a seasoned turnaround expert with an impressive track record, Mark had never worked in the energy storage devices industry. He knew boards typically prefer industry veterans.

Energon

Energon had been around for eight years. Started as an engineering shop, the company evolved into a technology innovator in energy storage devices.

Sales had grown fast, hitting $100 million in sales in only five years. Energon took advantage of the initial wave of adoptions of its devices by a first generation of applications, driven primarily by subsidies for renewable energy. In the beginning, the company enjoyed substantial margins. This prompted competitors to enter the market, which drove prices down.

Around the same time, subsidies for the sector started to be phased out sooner than expected. As a result, Energon's revenues dropped by 50% over the three years that followed.

This drop caught the company off guard, resulting in significant excess capacity and high fixed costs, which led to an extremely high cash burn rate. The former CEO convinced the board the drop was temporary and that the market would soon correct. But a reversal never occurred. By the third year, Energon had burned through much of its cash reserves.

The company's lenders were nervous. Energon had only three months of cash left and the board, under pressure from these lenders, was forced to fire the CEO. He seemed incapable of grasping the urgency of the situation and taking action—fast.

Finding and hiring a new CEO wasn't an easy task. Under normal circumstances, it would have taken six months to conduct a comprehensive executive search. But Energon didn't have six months; it had three at most.

Internally, employee morale was dropping fast. Energon's survival was at stake. That was when the lender suggested bringing in an interim CEO.

The Interim CEO

Mark Whitman was not new to turnarounds. If he got the job, Energon would be his seventh turnaround in 12 years. He'd been frequently retained as an interim CEO, tasked with taking a company in distress from the brink of bankruptcy to a successful recovery. His engagements lasted, on average, 12 to 24 months. Once the companies were on solid ground with a competent management team and improving finances, he'd move on to the next turnaround.

Mark started his adult life in the military. After completing two tours of duty in the armored corps as an officer, he went to college and graduated with a master's degree in electrical engineering. This gave him the opportunity to start his professional career as a research and development (R&D) engineer and work on defense and aerospace projects.

Mark liked being an engineer for a while, but he moved into sales as soon as an opportunity presented itself. He was convinced that being on the revenue-generating side of the business would give him a new perspective.

He got his first taste of a turnaround when he was promoted from head of sales to replace the CEO of a struggling business. He was so successful at the job that he was eventually asked to take on another turnaround. This became a pattern for the next 12 years.

After his third turnaround, Mark took a break and went back to school, spending a year at Stanford Business School to earn a master's degree in business administration. He was 40 years old at the time and probably the oldest student in the class. To others, it may have seemed odd that he'd go back to school after already building an impressive résumé. But he did it to learn unfamiliar business fundamentals, to reflect on what he had done well and where he had struggled, and to understand the reasons behind his successes and failures.

His studies exposed him to new management ideas and tools, which he later applied to turnarounds with great success. It also exposed him to a network of colleagues and friends he could turn to as sounding boards when faced with challenges he didn't know how to address.

Due Diligence

Before agreeing to consider the position at Energon, Mark asked for background information on the company and its industry. In particular, he wanted to talk to the CTO (Chief Technology Officer) so he could understand if Energon's technology offered a competitive advantage and whether new competitors would face significant barriers to entry.

Robert Williams, the CTO, was a technology whiz. A PhD with deep knowledge of advanced materials, he explained how proud Energon was to offer the best technology on the market, even though it wasn't always used to its fullest extent in current applications. Energon products can withstand extreme conditions, he told Mark, making them costlier to produce but delivering far better features than those of its competitors.

Mark also spent a significant amount of time researching Energon's existing and potential markets. He recognized that if the company didn't have or could not achieve product-market fit in the short term, the chances of a successful turnaround would be slim.

Product-market fit meant being in a large enough market with a product that can satisfy that market.[3]

Based on what he heard from Robert, he made a couple of phone calls to his old friends in the defense industry as well as to his former Stanford classmates. Soon enough, he identified three promising new applications for Energon's technology and decided to investigate further.

He also thoroughly studied the company's previous three years' financial statements and learned everything he could from the biographies of those on the management team.

---

[3]   Term defined by Marc Andreessen, an American entrepreneur, investor, and software engineer. He is the co-author of Mosaic, the first widely used Web browser; co-founder of Netscape; and co-founder and general partner of Silicon Valley venture capital firm Andreessen Horowitz.

A Reluctant Chairman

Will arranged a call between Mark and James, the chairman of Energon, which started awkwardly. The lender suggested Mark to the chairman while putting pressure on the board to take immediate action.

James believed no person inexperienced in the industry could address the issues Energon was facing. It became immediately clear he had little confidence in Mark's ability to deal with Energon's root problems. Instead, it felt like a courtesy call to appease the lender.

"Why do you think you are the right person to help Energon?" asked James.

"I never said I was the right person," said Mark. "But I took time to do some homework on your company, and I'm happy to share my conclusions."

"That would be interesting to hear," said James.

Mark began, "The first thing I did was investigate your current market and do research about Energon's product-market fit. It seems the entire industry is in turmoil. All the market participants have cornered themselves in the same segment, probably because it was growing quickly and had attractive margins. But now they are all suffering and can't escape due to limitations with their technology. Energon has a unique advantage that will allow it to access new, higher-margin market segments with serious barriers to entry that other competitors will face.

"Second, I called some of my contacts and validated the customers' pain, the pricing levels, and the market size. Based on the information I gathered, the most important factor for Energon's recovery is to achieve product-market fit in a short timeframe and identify additional markets for future expansion. I believe this is possible."

"This is the first time I'm hearing this," said James. "How did you conclude that we have a unique technological advantage?" he asked.

"I had a few calls with your CTO, and he explained the recent breakthroughs you'd achieved in extreme conditions applications. Thanks to my background in power electronics, I understand and appreciate the strong differentiating factors your technology provides that would have addressed problems I encountered as an R&D engineer in defense and aerospace."

"So, what's the path to recovery for the company?" James asked, sounding suddenly hopeful.

"From the limited information I've received and my research of public data, I believe the company should reposition itself as a high-quality manufacturer with premium pricing and then diversify into extreme conditions applications. To fund that effort in the short term, you'd have to sell off some of your ancillary product lines," Mark advised.

"Hmm, I hadn't thought of that," said James. "And I wasn't aware of the extreme conditions differentiator. What would you do first to make this work?"

Mark explained the steps he would take, with milestones at 30, 90, and 180 days.

Clearly impressed, the chairman told him, "Let me take your ideas to our board members and get their feedback."

The Job

After two months and five additional interviews with various members of the board and staff, Mark was wondering if he was still being considered for the job of Interim CEO at Energon. Frankly, after all this time, he thought the chances of landing the job where slim. And still present was the issue of payment and cash runway—the amount of time they had before running out of money.

As a turnaround CEO, Mark is usually paid months in advance due to the high risk of default posed by businesses in distress. He is also not cheap and the more is at stake, the greater his value and price. It would not be unusual for him to be paid 7 figures a year for a turnaround like Energon. He would also ask as part of his compensation significant equity in the business. This would guarantee a stake in the outcome and would align him with the interests of the shareholders. For him to implement the required changes, he needed enough cash to keep the company afloat until the results of his actions started generating free cash flow. Providing pre-payment and runway signaled a commitment from lenders and shareholders willing to invest in the recovery of the company. Mark simply didn't know if they'd be willing to make such a commitment and accept his price.

And then the phone rang.

"Hi, Mark. It's Will. Listen, buddy, it looks like Energon agreed to our terms. The board seems to have run out of options and the chairman wants you to start next week."

"Next week?" Mark asked. "But I made other plans. After so much time interviewing, I thought we'd lost momentum, and they weren't in enough pain to act."

"Well, it seems the situation has continued to deteriorate. The lender put Energon on notice that it will foreclose on its loan unless the company makes changes to the board, appoints you as Interim CEO and raises a bridge round from the existing investors to give you the 6 months of runway you asked for."

"Hmm. Interesting. And what is now the post money valuation of the company?" asked Mark

"Is twenty million. Only two investors agreed to put more money and the others were practically washed out." said Will

"That's quite a drop-in value from 3 years ago. If I remember well they were valued at $150m" said Mark

"OK. What about the first installment on my contract. Did they pay?"

"Yes, the money is in the bank," Will reassured him.

"Then let me move things around in my schedule."

Observe-Orient-Decide-Act

Agility

Mark learned the hard way that agility is the key to the success of any turnaround. Agility means acting fast based on quick decisions taken in a rapidly changing environment.

Previously, he entered a turnaround with pre-conceived ideas and got bogged down in a rigid bureaucracy. By the time he figured that out, it was too late. His former military training in the armored corps exposed him to the use of agility in maneuver warfare, but it took him a while to connect the dots to business situations.

The idea of operating at a quicker time pace than one's opponent was a central part of his training. It was based on the Observe-Orient-Decide-Act or OODA Loop, a revolutionary idea introduced by a brilliant military strategist in the United States Air Force named John Boyd.[4]

This concept stated that decision-making occurs in a recurring cycle of observe-orient-decide-act. An organization that can process this cycle quickly by observing and reacting to unfolding events more rapidly than an opponent can "get inside" the opponent's decision cycle and gain the advantage

---

[4]   See Appendix: The OODA Loop

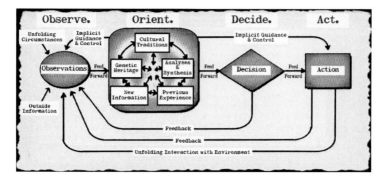

Figure 1 - John Boyd's description of the OODA Loop

Mark learned that the most important step in the OODA Loop was Orient. That's where mental models exist, and mental models form how everything in the OODA Loop works. Orientation shapes the way we interact with the environment—the way we observe, the way we decide, the way we act.

In a business environment, the dominant force shaping the Orient step is a company's culture. The invisible hand of its culture enforces a set of implicit norms of behavior.

The Orient step is critical to the pace of the OODA Loop. A good Orient step will be informed by the company culture and will allow skipping an explicit Decision step by providing Implicit Guidance & Control. The explicit decision-making step is time consuming, yet the biggest risk in a turnaround is losing time due to always trying to be explicit.

How well one's orientation matches the real world is largely a function of how carefully one observes. Anything that restricts the inflow of information or ideas can lead to disorientation between what one *thinks* is happening and what *is* happening, thus delaying any ability to take action.

So how does one get oriented in a rapidly changing environment? By constantly breaking apart old paradigms and putting the resulting pieces into a new perspective that better matches the current reality. But that's easier said than done . . .

Culture

Mark was acutely aware that the most important factor in creating agility was shaping a new culture. Because culture is the invisible actor that hides behind implicit behavior, creating a Culture By Design (as opposed to a Culture By Accident) became his top priority.

And he knew it all started with language and rituals.

Why language? Because language matters. Research has shown that humans' ability to discern colors depended largely on the cultural context in which they are raised—that is, human brains cannot distinguish colors when no names exist for them. Thus, language informs the way we think and interact with the world.

Company culture has a similar relationship with language. From mission statements to taboos on certain words, the language of an organization shapes its culture, and its culture shapes its people's actions.

Mark was envisioning that remote or mobile workers would soon join the company. Based on previous experiences, he knew culture was crucial, and building the right culture becomes a challenge when everyone isn't under the same roof anymore. More and more, workers from across industries and generations were working from home. He personally embraced home offices as an extension of the BYOD

(Bring Your Own Device) movement. It reduced infrastructure and overhead demands while blending elements of the mobile freelancer with a permanent workforce.

Because of mobile workers, neither the work nor the workspace served as an effective pillar of company culture. Mobile technology was giving people and their organizations more flexibility in where and how they work, while simultaneously disrupting how tasks were assigned, connected, and accomplished. In the mobile context, shared spaces, shared responsibilities, and shared resources could no longer be taken for granted. Therefore, with all this potential for disconnection and silo formation, a shared language was the most powerful way to keep workers culturally united.

Mark knew that linguistic differences, more than numbers, could lead to profound changes in emotional understanding, especially in distressed situations such as turnarounds.

Why rituals? A ritual is a universal feature of human existence. Just as we can't envision a society without language, we couldn't imagine a society without ritual. In fact, it's an inevitable component of culture, extending from the largest-scale social and political processes to the most intimate aspects of individual experience.

What Mark thought about ritual occurs throughout "modern" society: collective experiences. The dictionary would explain it as "done in accordance with social custom or normal protocol."[5]

Company culture was for Mark the collective experience he should enable to achieve his goals. The goal was to achieve Implicit Guidance & Control to speed up the OODA loop cycle in the direction of his strategic intent.

---

[5]   Merriam Webster Dictionary

He knew the heart of a ritual is rhythm. In the words of leading business expert Jeff Sutherland, "Rhythm is deeply important to human beings. Its beat is heard in the thrumming of our blood and rooted in some of the deepest recesses of our brains. We're pattern seekers, driven to seek out rhythm in all aspects of our lives."[6]

---

[6]   Sutherland, Jeff; Sutherland, JJ. *Scrum: The Art of Doing Twice the Work in Half the Time* (p. 85). The Crown Publishing Group. Kindle Edition.

Decoding Human Behavior

Observe People

During his first two weeks at Energon, Mark had intensive one-on-one meetings with his leadership team and with middle managers. He also participated in calls with customers.

From his research, he knew Energon would be a challenging turnaround, but this one seemed different than previous assignments. All the employees seemed discouraged, unsure of what—if anything—management was doing about the situation. No one at the top was talking to them, so they began to picture worst-case scenarios, including manufacturing lines being shut down due to lack of orders. If there was a potential solution, no one had shared it with them. They felt left out.

Despite the gloomy atmosphere, Mark resolved not to succumb to pessimism. He knew that any situation was typically not as bad, or as good, as it initially appeared. In fact, he showed a strange calm when things got bad—a habit he acquired in military training and tested under fire in battle. He knew that people would look to him for guidance and leadership, and his body language would be the main communicator.

Mark was mostly interested in observing the organizational dynamics and the friction preventing the company from seeing the light at the end of the tunnel. He knew he had little time to figure things out but resisted the urge to start barking orders at everyone just to feel in control. That wouldn't help, he knew.

He could feel the distrust between departments as information exchanges ground to a halt. Little was shared internally. No information was kept in sight, and reports were circulated through email as attachments, but no one knew if anyone was actually reading them.

Mark was puzzled by the apparent disconnect between team performance and the skills and experience of team members. Organizations he'd worked for typically went to great lengths to hire the best, only to see them fail. He had learned early how critical it is for a newly appointed leader to quickly know all the people on the team as if going through a mental "re-hiring" process to see who should stay and who needs to go. The usual information available was a bio page or maybe a résumé.

Before each scheduled meeting with a team member, Mark had less than 10 minutes to prepare. So he read through résumés quickly, looking at the last jobs they'd held and their education, and he formed opinions quickly. He was looking at their "Briefcase"— their education, knowledge, skills, and experience—what they bring to work every day. More often than not, he'd discover he had a highly experienced, well-educated team. But their résumés did not correlate with the actual business results he was brought in to achieve.

Many leaders pride themselves on their ability to read people. Studies show that you make a hiring decision within the first six seconds of meeting them based on a gut reaction. Then during the rest of the meeting, you look for evidence to support that decision. However, research has shown that the success rate in predicting future performance from unstructured interviews is a terrible 6%.[7]

---

[7] Source: Predictive Index

Why was the failure rate so high? What was missing?

Since the beginning of his career, Mark was curious about why people behave as they do. He'd had his first taste of behavioral science 20 years before as a candidate for a job. He wasn't particularly interested in the job at the time because he was happy with his current employer, but he went to the interview anyway. And he was blown away by the company's recruitment process. In particular, as part of the hiring activities, he was asked to complete the Predictive Index Behavioral Assessment (PI).[8]

What Mark found especially powerful was hearing the results of the assessment that his future boss shared with him. The assessment took five minutes and involved no questions to answer nor any multiple-choice responses. It simply consisted of a list of words in his native language for him to select from.

From this list of words came an incredibly accurate prediction of Mark's behavior. But what was even more interesting was that his future boss shared his own behavioral profile and, suddenly, the mask was off. From there, they explored how his future boss could set Mark up for success in ways that matched his needs.

Behavioral science had taught Mark that he was missing information about hearts and minds. One's heart was about values; one's mind was about drives and cognitive ability. But that kind of information was not on anyone's résumé, and any observable behavior from a brief interview couldn't provide a good sample to judge from.

---

[8]   The Predictive Index Behavioral Assessment® is a tool that predicts primary personality characteristics of a person predicting workplace behaviors and on-the-job performance. See Appendix.

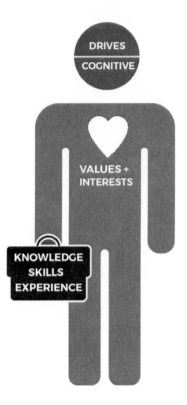

Mark learned that actions begin with drives, and some drives people are born with. For example, everyone has the innate drive to survive while other drives result from heredity, experience, or learning.

Drives create needs, and we behave in response to our needs. The drive to survive causes us to feel a need to eat food every day. The need to eat food (being hungry) causes us to walk across the street to get a sandwich. The drive creates a need and the need results in observable behavior.

However, the same behavior may be the result of different drives and needs. Say you stop at the same sandwich shop every morning to grab some coffee. Every time, you see a table of senior citizens talking and laughing. Are they there because they are hungry? I think it's something else. What might it be? Need for companionship? A sense of belonging? Clearly, they have the same behavior but a different need than you do.

One could probably identify the group's needs by studying their observable behavior over time. But as a turnaround manager, Mark knew he didn't have time on his side. He could only take advantage of identifying people's needs if he could quickly identify them using a tool.

The Leadership Team

From the lender, Mark had received the leadership team bios and "color" prior to starting at Energon. He studied their "Briefcases" and Googled the team's profiles for more details. He also asked around and got feedback from the chairman and other board members about each manager. From what he could see, they all had impressive credentials.

John Smith, Chief Financial Officer

The role of chief financial officer was an interesting one when investment interest was high. John knew that better than anyone; he had helped the company raise impressive amounts of money in his previous role at a prestigious investment banking firm. He was asked to join Energon as CFO five years before, and when the former CEO was fired, John became the acting CEO. One of the board's favorites, John was considered for the permanent CEO job but was ultimately not selected due to opposition from the lender. It seems he had been tasked with containing costs and proved unable to do that. Still, he had a natural ability to socialize and make people like him. John had earned an MBA from an Ivy League university and started his career in investment banking directly out of school.

Jerry Gold, Sales

Jerry was an outside hire who brought with him a lot of sales experience. He had previously worked for several semiconductor manufacturers, mainly in high-volume, low-cost market segments. He put himself through college on a sports scholarship and started his career as a sales engineer, rising through the ranks with hard work and persistence.

A strong personality, Jerry was protective of his turf and would blame any drops in sales on the high price of the product. His favorite method to push sales was through end-of-quarter promotions and discounts. The consensus was that Jerry fought hard to be the next CEO.

Robert Williams, Chief Technology Officer

A top scientist with a PhD in advanced materials from a famous technical university, Robert has been with Energon for 10 years. He brought with him the know-how regarding development of the energy storage devices product line. Robert had formed a remarkable team of top scientists and engineers who looked up to him, and he was well known throughout the industry for his deep knowledge and creative approaches to technical challenges.

Michael Jones, Director of Production

Energon's most senior employee after 24 years with the company, Michael previously worked in another division that was recently divested. Under Michael's leadership, the division was able to cut its lead time by 30% and reduce waste by 20%. He believed he was doing what he could, but the current situation had him quietly considering early retirement.

Behavioral Science at Work

During their first meeting, Mark asked John, the CFO, to take the Predictive Index Behavioral Assessment (PI). He said, "I'd like to continue this conversation next week to focus on getting to know each other better. We'll need to interact frequently in the coming weeks, and I want to better understand your needs and share mine so we can work together more effectively.

"I'm using a short behavioral assessment called the Predictive Index to facilitate this conversation. The assessment will take you five minutes tops. I will send you a link this afternoon so you can take the assessment before our meeting tomorrow."

"Sounds good to me," John replied, not feeling sure what to expect.

The next day, Mark printed out John's assessment report and headed to their meeting.

"Good morning. Ready to dive in?" asked Mark.

"Sure," answered John. The two men sat down facing each other.

"First," said Mark, "I'd like to tell you about the assessment you just completed. It's called The Predictive Index Behavioral Assessment, and it measures inherent drives that are present in all people to some degree. It predicts that people will behave in ways that meet their needs. It's scientifically proven that when people's needs are met at work, productivity, loyalty, engagement, and performance increase."

"That makes sense," replied John.

"We can also understand how the pressures of the environment are affecting you and how you try to adapt . . . and here is what it says," said Mark, looking at John's behavioral pattern.

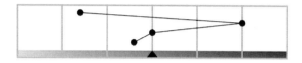

Figure 2 - John's PI Pattern

"You are socially focused and you will quickly and naturally empathize with other points of view and emotions. You will be positive, accepting communication designed to reduce conflict and increase interpersonal harmony," Mark read from the report.

"How am I doing so far, John?" asked Mark.

"It's a good start," said John, nodding his head and smiling.

"You are open in sharing information about yourself and what you know. You need a collaborative environment where you can be a big help; rarely saying 'no' when asked for something. You put your team and company goals before your own and you will promote teamwork by widely sharing authority," Mark continued reading.

"You are relatively informal and outgoing with others. You communicate in an open, lively, flexible manner, drawing others into the conversation. You are more interested in people, building relationships, and teamwork than technical matters. You are generally affable, optimistic, and trusting.

"You are focused on goals and the people you need to get there, and are comfortable delegating details," said Mark.

"Wow, this is truly me," said John. "And you got all this from a five-minute assessment? So now tell me the bad news."

"Interesting you say that," answered Mark. "You assume I delivered only the good news, because you recognize yourself and you *like* yourself. There is no good or bad news in a behavioral pattern. Think of it as the context that will provide a good fit for your behavioral drives. But in itself, a behavioral pattern simply describes your comfort zone, which would ideally be enabled by the environment you chose to live and work in."

"Very interesting," said John, sitting back in his chair. "So how will you use this information with me?"

"Well, this pattern tells me what you need, and I'll try to provide it. Here's what I believe you need," Mark continued. "You need opportunities for frequent contact and communication with others, particularly in a helpful role. You need individual and group recognition, especially for teams and relationships you've built. You need coaches, mentors, or trusted advisors. And you need a stable work environment and team."

"If this could happen, it would really make me happy," said John.

"Now, let me tell you what *I* need," said Mark, showing John his own pattern.

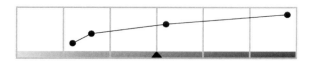

Figure 3 - Mark's PI pattern

"According to my PI Assessment, I need to see and feel a fast-moving and aggressive pursuit of goals. I'm eager to delegate details and implementation plans, leaving me to focus on new ideas," he explained.

"I am sometimes reluctant to delegate true authority, but I will eagerly discuss ideas with others, and I enjoy the process. However, my inner convictions are extremely strong, and I will need compelling arguments to change my mind," he said.

"My follow-up is quick and cursory; I'm likely to consider detailed minutia impediments to focusing on the big picture. I've already learned that I need to work with people who would be able to rigorously analyze and act on the details to keep me out of trouble.

"I constantly look to improve performance and our ability to compete, and I'm willing to try radical new solutions and innovative approaches. That's why I encourage others to look at things from entirely new perspectives. I will be relentless in the pursuit of change and creativity," Mark explained.

"I will be direct, spontaneous, and opinionated, and I will quickly voice my opinions of how things are going," he concluded.

"Well, that's really good to know," said John. "I've never had others explain so clearly what they need. It certainly makes life easier. Thank you for sharing with me."

That day, Mark went through the same process with the rest of his leadership team and got a good idea of his team's current behavioral fit.

Predicting Behavior

Next morning, reviewing the PI results of his management team, Mark already knew he'd face trouble.

His first concern was John. In turnarounds, one needs to run a tight ship. Financials need to be precisely measured and delivered almost in real time. For John, PI predicted that "his follow-up will be casual and cursory" and "Informal in style, John will be fairly casual about strict adherence to company policy, or the precise accuracy of the details of his work, preferring to delegate details to others."

John was not an assertive person. He preferred to avoid conflict and delay making critical decisions when he could not reach a consensus. But Mark had no time for consensus at this stage. With John's behavioral drive, it was no mystery he was running a lax financial department. And that was part of the problem.

His second concern was Jerry. In a normal situation, Jerry's behavioral drives would position him well to become the next CEO. But now was a time for tough choices. There were unpopular decisions to make, yet Jerry was highly sensitive to how other people perceived him. It was uncomfortable for him to ask customers to pay or to communicate price increases. He would also have a hard time firing people. Moreover, status was a big concern for Jerry. Any attempt to affect his status would be poorly received.

Robert was an excellent match for his role. The PI assessment predicted him to be an "intense, results-oriented, self-starter whose drive and sense of urgency are tempered and disciplined by his concern for the accuracy and quality of his work." Perfect for an action-oriented CTO!

In Michael's case, Mark knew he needed to be careful. He definitely wanted somebody in manufacturing to be "a thoughtful, disciplined person who is particularly attentive to, careful of, and accurate with the details involved in his job." But in times of chaos such as turnarounds, Michael would be stressed. Mark knew he needed to provide a setting where Michael would have the chance to learn and practice in an orderly way with "stability and predictability in his work environment and responsibilities."

(The Predictive Index Behavioral reports of the entire team are available in the Appendix.)

Culture By Design

A New Chapter

After a week of meeting people and observing behavior, Mark invited the top and middle managers to a meeting he called "A New Chapter."

"Hello, everybody," he greeted them. "It's been a week now since I started in this job, and I think it's time to establish ground rules on how we will work together. But before I ask anything, I would like to share my commitments to you:

- I am committed to **turn around** Energon.

- I am committed to **clarify** the vision and strategy of the company so you can use it and implement it in day-to-day activities.

- I am committed to **build** a Culture By Design. **How we do it** is as important to me as **what we do.**

- **I have zero tolerance for jerks**. If you think I am being a Jerk call me on it…

"I would also like to share with you who I am as expressed by my Behavioral Assessment Report.[9] The report is available to you in the

---

[9]   Mark's PI Behavioral Report can be found in the Appendix.

folder you received at the beginning of this meeting. It's also available to everybody for download on the company intranet."

Mark could sense the shock among the managers. This frank, direct style was new to them. Then he continued, "Now I'd like to tell you what I'm asking in return for my commitment.

- Deliver what **you** commit to.
- Don't ask for permission; **ask for forgiveness**
- Have a "healthy" disrespect for authority. Do what's best **for the company**, not what is good for your boss.
- Let yourself be judged by the **results of the team.**
- Don't make yourself irreplaceable. Nobody is!
- Don't be a hero; **balance your load.**

"Now, I'm happy to answer any questions, either professional or personal in nature."

Awkward silence. Then one person asked, "What does it mean 'don't be a hero; balance your load'?"

Mark replied, "It means I expect you to take care of yourself and work highly efficient eight-hour days. I prefer eight *effective* hours over twelve *heroic* hours. That's why it's important to me not only *what* we do but *how* we do it."

Moving from their initial shock to slight enthusiasm, the managers warmed up to Mark. The next question asked was, "Can you explain Culture By Design?"

"Sure," said Mark. "Culture By Design means purposely shaping our culture using carefully chosen language and rituals. The advantage of taking the time to clarify the language and implementing sound rituals is the ability to act faster with consistency in the strategic direction we chose to go to, and then allowing the culture to inform our day-to-day decisions. This contrasts with Culture By Accident in which our habits are randomly created without understanding their impact."

·With the audience warmed up, questions started to pour in. Everyone showed a genuine interest to do something about the company's situation.

Then 10 minutes before the top of the hour when the meeting would end, Mark said, "Before we adjourn, I'd like to introduce a new ritual intended to get us in sync every morning before we move ahead with our daily activities.

"First, each one of you and your subordinates will be allocated to what we call Scrum Teams. Each team will have a maximum of eight people but not less then five. You'll find in your folders who is allocated to which teams. Each team has a coach called a Scrum Master, who will guide everyone to implement the Scrum method in our daily work.

"Tomorrow morning at nine-fifteen, each team will meet at a designated location to get briefed on what Scrum is. Then team members will run their first Daily Standup. *This is not rocket science.* You pass a ball and each person holding the ball answers these three short questions: *what did you do yesterday, what you will do today, and do you have any impediments?*

"And here's a critical detail. We call it a Daily Standup because *we all stand up.* This keeps the meeting short—no more than fifteen minutes."

A New Language

Mark gradually started to introduce new language in conversations and made sure people understood the differences with similar words used previously. That included conversations he'd had with the R&D team in the first product review meeting.

"Can you tell me what you are working on right now in R&D?" asked Mark

Robert took the lead and said, "We are now building a prototype for a new device we think will have good chances of adoption."

"Can you elaborate? What do you mean by 'prototype'?" asked Mark.

"Hmm, I didn't think about what we mean by this. I guess a **prototype** is an early model of a future product to test the concept with customers," replied Robert.

"And what are you trying to do with this particular prototype?" asked Mark.

"Well, we would like to show it around and see if anybody would be interested in it," answered Robert.

"Got it," said Mark. "I'd like to tell you I have a strong preference to develop products that are already connected to specific markets, and we have a way to test the minimal requirements that would make a customer buy the product. It's about the bare minimum that would make a customer try it. I call this the **Minimal Viable Product or MVP**."

"Hmmmm. I think I understand the distinction. I never thought of it in these terms. Very well, then MVP it is," said Robert. From then on, he used this new acronym in all his meetings and reports.

Mark made sure that a dictionary of similar new terms became available online to the entire company for reference. And when he used a new term in his emails, he would include a link to the definition of the term.

Gradually, Mark would be surprised when employees he never met started to use these new terms in conversations with him. He knew the success of introducing a new language is like Drip Irrigation. That's when you introduce a new term and use it consistently while explaining its meaning every time until it becomes second nature. Still, you make sure you do not overwhelm users with too many terms. Introducing new language gradually is key.

Almost imperceptibly, new terms became part of the day-to-day language at Energon. For example, instead of Mark hearing about Initial Sales, he'd hear the term Minimal Viable Traction (MVT) or instead of Project Manager, he'd hear Scrum Master.

A New Ritual

The next day at 9:15, members of the management team showed up in the main meeting room with their coffee mugs. After sitting down around the meeting table, Mark greeted them by saying, "Now, if you're ready to start the Daily Standup, you might remember we said we'd stand so we have no temptation to do anything except report on the three questions."

After everyone stood up, Mark passed around a ball to be held as each person gave a report. He started first.

"Yesterday, I had a New Chapter meeting with the entire management team. I also had a meeting with the lender to learn about the foreclosure forbearance. Today, I will meet individually with each one of you to discuss your 'quick win' ideas. I have no impediments." Then he passed the ball to the closest team member, saying, "Whoever holds the ball will start reporting. When you are done, pass the ball to somebody else."

Michael had the ball so he stated his report and the others followed in this way: "Yesterday I . . . ; today I will . . . ; I am blocked by . . ."

The whole Daily Standup took 12 minutes. As he adjourned the Daily Standup, Mark said, "I hope you all go back to your activities feeling more in sync with your team members."

A New Mental Model

Mark was used to doing back-of-the-envelope calculations to play with simple economic models that would provide a roadmap for the economic side of a turnaround. He was convinced if he couldn't fit a model on a back of an envelope, it wouldn't be simple enough to be communicated and executed.

In Energon's case, he imagined a model that could swing EBITDA[10] from -10m to +7m in the following 12 months. Theoretically, all the initiatives would be possible with no (or little) investment.

Mark's economic turnaround principle was simple.

	Impact on Revenue	Impact on EBITDA	Balance
Current Ops	$50m	$10m	$10m
Current Fixed Costs		($20m)	($10m)
Cut Fixed Costs		$10m	$0
Discontinue Products	($20m)	($4m)	($4m)
Increase Prices 30%	$8m	$8m	$4m
Add High Margin/ Low Volume	$6m	$3m	$7m

---

[10] Earnings before interest, tax, depreciation, and amortization (**EBITDA**) is a measure of a company's operating performance.

Address gross margin. Identify products with gross margins less than 20% and kill them.

Identify the group of products used in less price-sensitive applications and increase their price by 30%. (This price increase minus some loss of revenue should directly increase EBITDA.)

The next step would be identifying opportunities to reduce capacity including disposal of assets. Following that is launching a product line for high margin/low volume segments based on the extreme conditions differentiation provided by Energon's unique technology.

Walk the Talk

Mark was a very punctual person. Naturally, he noticed when people were regularly late for meetings. It was clear this was part of the culture and not an accident. However, nobody seemed to be bothered that others were late and meetings would regularly start and end late.

So he picked a meeting with his management team when half of them were late to the meeting and said, "Guys, being late for meetings does not work for me. I would like to suggest a fun way to fix this. Let's institute a Party Fund, and whoever is late to a meeting contributes to the fund. How much should we ask for a late incident?"

His team listened in disbelief but then realized Mark was dead serious about this fund. So they came up with a number—$5 every incident—and verbally agreed to playing the game.

"OK, then to make this happen, we need to have a timekeeper for every meeting. At the beginning of the meeting, on the whiteboard, we'll first assign a notetaker and a timekeeper. The timekeeper will record the 'late incidents' in a Late Incidents database and announce when the meeting has ten minutes left.

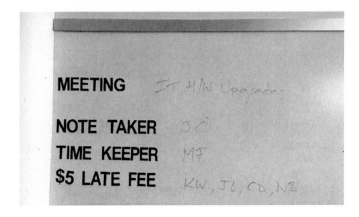

Mark volunteered to be timekeeper for the first couple of meetings. He also made sure a dashboard with the Late Incidents was displayed on a TV in the lobby.

"What is this Late Incidents Screen?" asked an employee one day walking through the lobby.

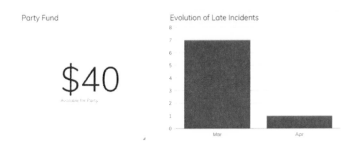

"Oh, that's the number of times members of the management team showed up late to meetings," said the receptionist with a smile. "And they pay five dollars each time they are late . . . "

Then came the day when Mark arrived late to a meeting. He immediately said, "I am late and I am sorry. Please hit me with five dollars. I want to transfer the money now to the Party Fund."

He was walking the talk . . .

Action

Backlog Grooming

Mark was exposed to agile software development while running a turnaround for a software company. He was amazed by the increase in productivity and focus that SCRUM, one of the agile development methods in the agile toolkit, brought to the company. Since then he used SCRUM in non-software development businesses with great success.

In the following two weeks, the entire company was broken down in agile teams of seven to nine members under the guidance of a Scrum Master.[11] That person, provided by an external adviser, helped the teams put together a list of key initiatives to drive the turnaround. These initiatives are called user Stories[12] while a list of stories is called a Backlog.[13]

---

[11] A **Scrum Master** is the facilitator for an Agile development team. **Scrum** is a methodology that allows a team to self-organize and make changes quickly in accordance with agile principles. The **Scrum Master** manages the process for how information is exchanged. See tools/Scrum in Appendix.

[12] A user **Story** is a high-level definition of a requirement, containing just enough information so the developers can produce a reasonable estimate of the effort to implement it. See tools/Scrum in Appendix.

[13] **Scrum Product Backlog** is a list of all things that needs to be done within the project. It replaces the traditional requirements specification artifacts. See tools/ Scrum in Appendix.

Each company team was also appointed a Product Owner[14] who would accept and prioritize Stories before they would be allocated to a two-week Sprint.[15]

At the beginning, each team committed 30% of its time in a week to work on Backlog grooming.[16] That meant coming up with Stories that could have an immediate impact on cash flow. The Product Owner and the team would review items on the Backlog to ensure it contains the appropriate items, that they are prioritized based on the value they would bring if implemented, and that the top items are ready for scheduling.

Team members would regularly play Estimation Poker[17] to align the team and size the Stories. In the estimation sessions, they'd reassess the relative priority of Stories and assign an estimate to Stories that didn't have one. Then they'd remove user Stories that were no longer relevant and create new user Stories in response to newly discovered needs.

After about three Sprints, the Backlogs reached substantial maturity and the results came quickly.

---

[14] A Scrum **Product Owner** is typically a project's key stakeholder. Each **Product Owner** has a vision of what he or she wants to build and conveys that vision to the Scrum team. See tools/Scrum in Appendix.

[15] A Sprint is a time-box of one month or less during which a "done," useable, and potentially releasable product increment is created. Sprints have consistent durations throughout a development effort. A new Sprint starts immediately after the conclusion of the previous Sprint.

[16] **Backlog grooming** is when the **Product Owner** and some or all the team members review items on the **Backlog** to ensure it contains appropriate items, that they are prioritized, and that the items at the top are ready for delivery. See Tools/Scrum in Appendix.

[17] **Planning Poker**, also called Scrum **Poker**, is a consensus-based, gamified technique for **estimating**, mostly used to **estimate** effort or relative size of development goals in software development. See Tools/Scrum in Appendix.

Increasing the Pressure

Friction was building as Mark increased the pressure for action. Specifically, he pushed John and Jerry as a way to probe his suspicions they'd become major blockers.

One day, he called Jerry into his office and said, "We need a way to preserve and/or generate cash to fight another day. How about killing any product that has less than 10% contribution margin and increasing prices selectively on all the others by an average of 15%."

"But this is not possible," said a visibly alarmed Jerry. "We have commitments to our customers, and we cannot drop a bomb like that on them. We could immediately lose half of our sales. The competition is coming after us with aggressive pricing, and we can't afford to have a lower volume of sales."

"Can you show me what part of our revenue we would lose and what would be the lost contribution margin?" Mark asked.

"We can't calculate a per product margin because it would be too complicated. We can calculate an average margin, and that stands at around 20% today," replied Jerry.

"This sounds to me like a joke about averages. If you keep your hands in a bucket with ice water and you sit on a burning stove, your hands might freeze and your ass might be burning, but on average your temperature is okay.

"So telling me the 'average' is not a good enough fact for me. I will tell John that we need to have margins calculated per product by the end of this week. But I want to see the price increases implemented this week."

Showing his nervousness, Jerry couldn't contain his anger. "This is the worst possible course of action. I don't know I can do that in less than a week anyway," he protested.

"I insist you do it *by the end of the week,*" replied Mark and adjourned the meeting.

Then he called John and said, "Jerry told me we can't calculate a per product margin because it would be too complicated. Is this true?"

John tried to explain how the on-premise accounting software wasn't flexible enough to drill down into individual margins. A while back, they had assumed it would be good enough to estimate an average gross margin. Moreover, his IT manager said that to achieve this level of detail, we'd need a multimillion-dollar investment that would take a year to implement.

"John," Mark insisted, "I need to have margins calculated per product by the end of this week. Friday at three in the afternoon, I'm scheduling a meeting with you to get a full report."

Mark expected John wouldn't fight back on this. As PI predicted, fighting simply wasn't his nature. As expected, by Friday, the prices hadn't been increased nor the gross margin report delivered. Then the following Monday, Mark called Jerry into his office to get a report on the previous week's request.

"Jerry, did you communicate the price increases?" asked Mark.

"I'm sorry, but we had no time to do it. We had a lot of orders coming in, and we had some complaints to deal with. I also had to travel to meet Client X," said Jerry, avoiding Mark's eyes.

"I think I made it crystal clear that this was my number one priority. Is there anything I am missing?"

"No, it just couldn't be done at such a short notice. We have many customers, and we did not have the resources to do it last week," Jerry concluded.

Mark had seen this type of passive resistance often. It was time for him to take action.

Removing the Cork

Mark believed that organizations are all complex adaptive systems. In the words of Scrum author Jeff Sutherland, "The same things that move cells from one state to another are also what move people from one state to another. To change a cell, you first inject energy into the system. At first there's chaos, there seems to be no rules, everything is in flux. When you do this to organizations trying to change, people often freak out. They can't understand what's happening. They don't know what to do. But remarkably quickly, just like a cell, an organization settles into a new steady state. The only question is whether the new state is better than the old one."[18]

Adding to this analogy is comparing change to removing the cork from a champagne bottle. You shake the bottle before attempting to open it—that is, you inject energy. Then you extract the cork—remove the blocker—that sends it shooting into the ceiling with a loud bang. Once the pressure in the bottle wins over the resistance of the cork, the cork pops and the foam overflows until the liquid is poured into a glass and settles, ready to be savored.

Mark had confirmation that his two "corks" or energy blockers were Jerry and John. From their PI results, he knew what to expect from their behavioral drives and could see them unfolding

---

[18] Sutherland, Jeff; Sutherland, JJ. *Scrum: The Art of Doing Twice the Work in Half the Time* (p. 85). The Crown Publishing Group. Kindle Edition.

in day-to-day activities. John was too lax with finances and did little follow up, leaving it to his team to run the financial shop—clearly expected as a behavioral pattern. Mark saw Jerry's recent action as an additional confirmation point.

Mark felt it was time to take the bull by its horns for both Jerry and John, yet he feared disrupting the organization. Jerry seemed to "own" the clients, and John enjoyed good connections with investors and board members.

However, with Mark's experience with "irreplaceables," he harbored strong opinions about them. He recalled a quote from one of his friends: "The best time to fire an employee is the first time you think about it."

After failing to act fast enough to "remove the cork" in his earlier turnarounds, he'd learned the hard way that no one is irreplaceable—including him. He also believed the quicker the cork is removed, the better. He decided to fire John and Jerry almost on the spot.

When Mark called Jerry in the next morning, Jerry had no idea what was about to happen.

"Jerry, I decided it's time for us to let you go."

"Me? You've got to be kidding. Of all the people in the team, you think I am the one . . . " He didn't complete the thought. He just said, "Me?"

Mark expected Jerry to put up a fight. He was right.

"What is the reason for this?" Jerry demanded.

Calmly, Mark explained, "Jerry, you don't seem to be aligned with me on what needs to be done to turn this company around. But mostly you don't have a sense of urgency about it."

"You do not think I'm aligned? The problem is that *you* don't understand the situation."

As the words came out of his mouth, Jerry remembered the previous week's request and realized what was going on. He tried to clarify by saying, "What you're asking for is not possible and definitely not at the speed you want it to happen."

Still fighting, Jerry continued, "How do you think the board will react to me being fired? They know I brought all the clients you have today, and I am the only one who can *keep* these clients." Jerry was practically describing himself as irreplaceable.

"Jerry, this is not a conversation. It is *me* telling *you* that today is your last day with Energon. Mary from HR will provide you with all the paperwork."

Visibly shocked, Jerry stared at the table in front of him. Mark felt Jerry was coming to terms with the situation. He was wrong.

Backlash

Mark expected uncomfortable backlash from sacking Jerry, but he didn't expect it to come from the chairman of the board, who called him that evening.

"I just got off the phone with Jerry," said James in a serious tone.

"So I guess you heard I let him go," replied Mark.

James continued, "I'm concerned you're moving too fast and too radically. Look, Mark, you know I don't want to tell you how to do your job. But maybe you should take time to understand the nature of this business before you burn bridges."

Mark let a few moments pass before replying. He knew that sacrificing "a sacred cow" would put him in a difficult position with the board. With calm, he shifted into CEO tone.

"OK, what I'm about to say is *not* meant to be in any way rude or defensive."

"I appreciate that, Mark."

"You may not after you hear what I have to say," Mark continued.

The chairman forced a laugh. "OK, I'm sitting down."

"First, do not think I'm randomly firing people. Everything I do is purposeful and intentional. If *you* knew how to do what I'm trying to do, you wouldn't need me, right?"

"You are right."

"I honestly appreciate your concern, but you brought me in to save the company, and you need to give me the benefit of the doubt. The situation will get worse before it gets better. The status quo is not acceptable, and people in the company need to know it's *not* business as usual."

Mark went on, "Over the past six months, you've been very involved in the day to day, more so than most board chairmen. During that time, you watched the company spiral further and further into the red. You've hired me to pull the company out of it. I assume you still want the same thing, right?"

"Absolutely," the chairman responded.

"That's exactly what I want, too. But then you need to be prepared to accept the consequences. This won't be easy or pretty."

The chairman remained silent for a moment, then said, "OK, I hear you. I need this fixed. So you have my support, Mark."

Outmaneuvering

In almost all Mark's turnarounds, the information was tightly controlled by the Finance Department and usually IT was part of the control, too.

Under John was a chief accountant and an IT director. Both took advantage of the lax manner John ran the department to make themselves irreplaceable. Anticipating he could be on a collision course with this turf, Mark got prepared from the start. He began by outmaneuvering[19] the system.

Having previously worked with a fractional finance and accounting services firm that embraced information openness, Mark believed in taking advantage of the Cloud to set up interconnected apps. Using these apps, it would take hours instead of weeks or months to get Energon's financial records up and running.

Mark prepared this framework under the radar of John's Finance Department. Before long, he asked specific departments to use Cloud apps for low-risk processes such as travel expenses. Every second week, he'd introduce a new app and ensure that support was available to make the process work. In parallel, he asked the accounting firm to set up a fresh instance of a Cloud-based accounting app that could

---

[19]   Evade (an opponent) by moving faster or with greater agility. - Merriam Webster Dictionary

import and clean the entire accounting database in a week. It could also instantly sync it with apps already running at the right moment.

Mark also had a data warehouse and business intelligence tools preconfigured to analyze the accounting information once it became available.

In the meantime, he asked Finance Department personnel to produce certain reports, knowing they'd be a lot of work using the existing tools. He also put pressure on them to meet deadlines. Periodically, he asked the heads of IT and accounting why it takes so long to receive the information.

His goal? To send a signal that speed and accuracy of information are high priorities. He gave the team lots of opportunities to come up with solutions. And as he expected, he received only excuses.

The morning after John was let go, Mark called in the chief accountant and the IT manager, telling them their services were no longer needed. Immediately after, he called a meeting with the entire accounting and IT staff and prepared each one for a soft landing. The fractional accounting service providers moved into the building. For the next two weeks, they provided support for the team to go live with the remaining apps waiting to be turned on.

With that move, Mark had gained all the necessary information *in real time* to run the business.

Transformation

With Jerry out of the picture, Mark looked into reforming the Sales Department. For this, he asked a PI Certified Partner to run a behavioral and cognitive assessment of everyone in the sales team and then correlate the results with the historic performance of each sales person.

He also compared each sales person's pattern with what resulted from a Job Behavioral Description Alignment[20] session he'd had with the management team.

Mark expected to see a correlation. More than that, he was amazed how well the behavioral/cognitive combination predicted success.

---

[20]   The Predictive Index Job Assessment tool that can predict the ideal behavioral pattern of a job. See Appendix.

Name	Role	Behaviour		PI Fit	Cognitive		Cog Fit	Overall	% of Quota	Tenure (years)
		Job Model	Person	Green Yellow Red	Range (0-50)	Score	Green Yellow Red	Green Yellow Red		
Tim W	Outside Hunter			😊	17-23	23	😊	😊	134%	7
Paul M	Outside Hunter			😐	17-23	12	😕	😟	47%	1.5
Peter M	Outside Hunter			😊	17-23	33	😊	😊	87%	3
Stuart P	Outside Hunter			😊	17-23	21	😐	😐	66%	1
Susan S	Outside Hunter			😊	17-23	31	😊	😊	95%	2
Tracey D	Outside Hunter			😐	17-23	37	😊	😐	76%	2
Andrew L	Outside Hunter			😟	17-23	32	😊	😟	78%	5
Tim B	Outside Hunter			😊	17-23	37	😊	😊	201%	3
Michelle F	Outside Hunter			😐	17-23	36	😊	😐	78%	2
Kristi G	Outside Hunter			😊	17-23	32	😊	😊	127%	4
Tony A	Outside Hunter			😊	17-23	37	😊	😊	121%	4
Holly L	Outside Hunter			😟	17-23	22	😐	😟	40%	0.5

Like a surgeon who quickly sees where to cut to save a patient's life, he could clearly understand what to look for *and* take immediate action. In the next two months, he replaced all the sales people who weren't a good match for the role. He then recruited people who matched the behavioral and cognitive patterns he wanted and invested in their Customer Focused Sales Training.

He also promoted Mike Henderson, an excellent sales person who had the right behavioral profile to manage people. Mike became the sales director and went immediately through intensive sales management training.

Within the next quarter, the new team could see a clear trend of increased orders for high-margin products *and* the disappearance of the culture of price-driven sales.

Everyday Turnaround

The Off-Site

After the swift removal of the "corks," Mark knew he needed to soft land people in the rest of the organization and provide them clarity for the future. So he asked everybody who managed or led others to join him in a two-day off-site meeting. He chose a location close enough to the office to avoid expensive, time-consuming travel but far enough away to feel as if they went out of town.

The meeting was scheduled to start at 9:00 in the morning. By 8:45, everyone had arrived and all 20 were seated at a round table.

Mark greeted everyone by saying, "Good morning. I'd like to start these two days by saying a few words. I know times have been tough and confusing for many of you. We did what we had to do to prepare the ground for the rapid changes needed to set up this company for success. I can assure you that personnel changes are over. The team currently in place is the one we want to move things forward."

A huge sigh of relief could be sensed in the room.

Mark continued, "I brought you here so we can look together into the future and get clear on what to expect in the next six months. Let me say what I think we know at this point. We have an experienced technical and manufacturing team. We have superb technology. Yet, despite all that, we are bleeding cash and our sales are in free fall. It's obvious we need to change that.

"In my opinion, the business was blindsided by the unexpected drop in sales from the markets that had been so generous to this company before. But the fixed costs weren't reduced fast enough to compensate for the drop of revenue and compression in margins. Today, the company has no space to maneuverer because the only market we're in is experiencing a serious contraction.

"Now is the time to explain my approach to this turnaround and clarify the strategic intent of our future actions. I call this approach The Everyday Turnaround."

Business Model

"It all starts with the Business Model," continued Mark.

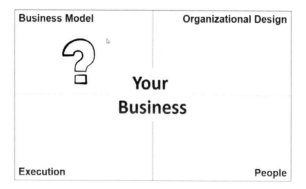

Business Model	Organizational Design
?	**Your Business**
Execution	People

Some people in the room were clearly needing an explanation.

Mark explained, "The Business Model is how do we think we will make money. In the Business Model, I am particularly interested in understanding the Product Market Fit. I don't believe in chances of recovery for any business that cannot achieve product market fit in a short time."

"What do you call product-market fit?" asked Robert.

"My interpretation of product/market fit is to have a product that's relieving a big enough pain or creating a big enough gain that people are willing to buy it at the right price AND that the market is big enough to be worth pursuing," said Mark.

"I looked at our product line, and I do not think we have a fit. And I would also say that we do not have a clear understanding of our place in the marketplace.

"A week ago, I asked our HR Department to run a survey using a tool called Line-of-Sight™[21] that's intended to identify the gaps in our Strategy to Execution capability. The survey reveals gaps in alignment across what the method calls the Keys to Strategy Execution.™ These keys are Strategic Understanding, Leadership, Balanced Metrics, Activities and Structure, Human Capital, and Market Discipline. The survey reveals if each key was aligned, misaligned, somewhat aligned, or not sure of alignment.

"I know you all received the invitation and took the survey. One of the questions in the survey measures the team's knowledge of our main competitors and how we differentiate from them. Take a look at the results," said Mark as he projected a slide showing the report.

---

[21]   Line-of-Sight is a trademark of Prana Business. All references to it are used with permission.

Measures our team's knowledge of our
main competitors and how we differentiate
ourselves from them

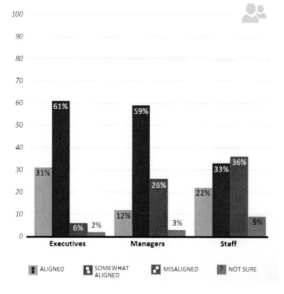

"Let me translate this chart for you. When a survey taker answers the question about the team's knowledge of the competition, the person is not only asked how well he or she knows the competition but asks about his or her confidence in the answer. This is than translated into a matrix called Confidence-Based Marking™[22] that tells the level of alignment with that statement.

---

[22]   A Trademark of Prana Business

"So, let's look again at the chart. You'll notice that the executive team has a 61% Somewhat Aligned and 31% Aligned result. But when you move one level below in the organization, you'll notice the middle management team is 21% Aligned and 59% Somewhat Aligned but, more important, 26% is Misaligned.

"The situation becomes more dramatic when we talk about the staff. At 36% Misaligned, 33% Somewhat Aligned, and only 22% Aligned, it's clear that what the executive team believes they understand about competition isn't communicated down the ranks. This means as an organization, we're mostly Misaligned on the subject of knowing our competition."

"This is a striking result," said Robert. "I didn't realize there's such a misalignment on a subject we all believed is a given."

"I actually fully agree with the result," said Michael. "I'm quite close to the manufacturing staff. Many times, we have no idea why certain changes in manufacturing are asked, and we just assume that's what is needed without asking too many questions."

"I'd like to ask a 'stupid' question, if I may," said Mark. "Can we increase the price?"

"Jerry was saying it's impossible," said Robert. "He was adamant that we're already considered the most expensive product in the market, and our competitors are eating our lunch."

"This would explain his behavior of pushing sales using discounts. Do you know why he was suggesting that?" asked Mark.

"His theory was that we were the first in the market with this product, and we enjoyed the first to market advantage for a couple of very good years. Since then, new competitors entered the market. Initially, they had inferior products and came with low prices that we could not compete with, so we tried to move upmarket. However, they closed the performance gap in about two years. All this happened when the existing market started to shrink."

"Ok, what about new products? Do we have any new products in the pipeline that would allow us to access new markets and charge a premium price?" Mark asked.

"We have some new technology that would allow us to create devices for extreme conditions," said Robert. "But we don't yet have a clear understanding of the required specs."

"It looks like we need to go back to the drawing board. I would like to brainstorm around our value proposition and potentially new business models," said Mark. "Robert, can you educate us about this new technology you mentioned earlier?"

"Of course. Our advanced materials present extremely good thermal conductivity and if mixed with other materials, they could be used as thermal interfaces. We are talking about one or two orders of magnitude increase in thermal conductivity."

Robert continued to explain how they could create a series of products for the electronics industry. These would be extremely disruptive in a market that was already above $1Bn and was poised to grow to $3Bn in the next five years.

"So, you're saying that we can imagine applications to extract heat out of electronic components where we can be a much better alternative to existing materials?" continued Mark.

"That's exactly what I'm saying," replied Robert.

It dawned on Mark that Energon owned intellectual property of exceptional value that would give them products for an entirely new market, but to make it happen, a new business model would be required. However, confusion existed about what type of strategy the company should pursue.

Mark moved on to clarify by saying, "I think it's important for us to decide what game we want to play. We need to have a common understanding of the possible options. I know that any strategy can be eventually categorized as one of these: Operational Excellence, Customer Intimacy, or Product Innovation."

In **Operational Excellence**, you want to deliver a combination of low price, ease, speed, hassle-free use, and convenience. This requires having streamlined processes that are optimized and standardized to remove variations. Operations need to be standardized, simplified, tightly controlled, and centrally planned, leaving few decisions to front-line employees. This requires a culture that looks down on waste and rewards efficiency with a mind-set of optimization, discipline, and process excellence.

The next option is **Customer Intimacy** in which you want to deliver customized products and services that solve specific problems or fulfill specific customer needs. Processes need to be loose and flexible, and they can enable solution development through customer relationships. As a result, you need to run your operations by delegating decision-making to employees. They work closely with customers and can act with little red-tape to allow for variations. Your systems are then geared toward creating specific results based on customer needs, including compensation systems that reward customer retention and enable customer knowledge. This requires a culture that embraces specific solutions and thrives on deep customer relationships. The organizational mind-set is focused on understanding the customer.

The final option is **Product Innovation**. This is about delivering innovative, cutting-edge, unique products or services. Basically, customers get the latest and greatest. This means you focus on invention, product development, and market exploitation. Operations will be loosely knit and constantly shifting. The mind-set will be entrepreneurial with a desire to work in unexplored territory. You will choose systems to measure and reward new product success without punishing experimentation and risk. You will need to allow and support variations that lead to innovation. This requires a culture that encourages imagination, out-of-the-box thinking with a mind-set driven by the desire to create the future.

After finishing his explanations, Mark asked, "What do you think our strategy type should be?"

"I think it's obvious we are a Product Innovation company," said Robert.

"Are you sure, Robert?" asked Mark.

"I'm pretty sure," he replied.

"Do you think our staff has the same opinion?" asked Mark.

A puzzled Robert took five seconds to think and then said, "I mean, it's quite obvious. I think people in our staff have the same opinion"

"Let me show you what Line-Of-Sight revealed. We asked, 'Our customers buy from us because our core strategy is . . . .' And big surprise, our staff thinks our strategy is Operational Excellence. Take a look at the results," said Mark.

"You can see how the executive team is sure is Product Innovation, but 75% of the staff thinks we have an Operational Excellence strategy," he continued.

Robert was visibly shocked by the result. Mark used the moment to make his point. "You can see now why debate and communication of strategy is a key responsibility of the executive team. You *cannot* overcommunicate strategy. This issue needs to be addressed immediately, so I suggest we spend one hour a day for the next month in strategy education and debate sessions to align the organization.

"Let's take a break now and come back in fifteen minutes to talk about what to do after we get clear about our Business Model," Mark concluded.

Execution Capability

Opening the next session, Mark asked, "How was the Business Model session for you?"

"Quite a shock for me," said Robert.

"Not a surprise for me," said Michael. "We're are under such pressure to shave every little cent to survive the pressure on margins that we had to take drastic measures to standardize and optimize all the manufacturing processes resulting in decreased flexibility"

Mark replied, "We need to make sure we have alignment across the organization on understanding our strategic intent so our strategy can inform day-to-day activities without explicitly instructing people what to do. And this needs to be reinforced by our capability to execute in the direction of the strategic intent.

"This brings me to the second step of the Everyday Turnaround. This is where we ask the question *Is our organization ready to execute effectively?*"

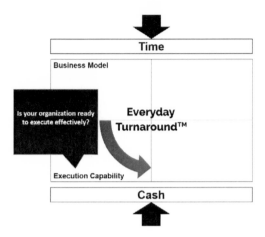

"But what is execution anyway?" Mark asked the group. After a couple of attempts to answer, Mark helped them by projecting a quotation on the screen.

Execution is a specific set of behaviors and techniques that companies need to master in order to have competitive advantage. It's a discipline of its own.[23]

"Hmm, quite concise I might say," commented Michael. "Can you elaborate on behavior and technique?"

"Of course. Let me use a military analogy," said Mike. "When you start your military service, you first learn all the rituals of the army. You learn to salute, to dress, to report back, to march in formation. Let's call this military behavior. Then you learn to fire your gun and take care of it. That would be a technique. Then the military would make you practice these continually until they become second nature to you. They become knowledge in your muscle memory."

---

[23]   *Execution: The Discipline of Getting Things Done* by Ram Charan and Larry Bossidy, Crown Business, 2002.

"Yes, that makes sense. I can see how that concept would work in a manufacturing environment," said Michael

"Well, I agree it's a necessary condition, but is it sufficient to achieve competitive advantage?" asked Mike. "I mean, I just described what probably every single army in the world does."

Those in the room felt like they'd reached an impasse. Mark broke the stalemate.

"What's missing are the hearts and minds of people. What makes an organization, military or business, superior in performance is its set of values and the rituals reinforcing those values."

"Could you elaborate on this please?" asked Robert.

"OK. Let me give you an example. The Israeli Air Force (IAF), arguably one of the best air forces in the world, considers its post-flight reviews[24] to be critical for the high performance level of its units. Those involved define what they learn in post-flight reviews as a process of retrospective sense-making, detection and correction of errors, social comparison, social control, socialization and bonding. This process is facilitated by the core values of the IAF: **Inquiry, Integrity, Transparency, Issue Orientation,** and **Accountability.** It assumes that **learning through critical examination** of one's own experience is the key to improvement," Mark explained.

"I just described a set of shared values and a ritual. The values are embedded in their culture and are called The Ethos of the IAF, an Ethos of Shared Responsibility. The Retrospectives are the rituals reinforcing those values on a daily basis.

---

[24] *How Organizations Learn: Post-flight Reviews in an F-16 Fighter Squadron.* Neta Ron, Raanan Lipshit, Micha Popper, Organization Studies, SAGE Publications, 2006.

"Now, you are able to relate to the Scrum Retrospectives we introduced a month ago. And the systematic effort to align the organization along the strategic intent of the company using Line-Of-Sight as a measuring tool."

"So, what is our role as managers in shaping this Execution Capability?" asked Robert.

"This is a perfect question," Mark responded. "You, as leaders of this organization at all levels, beyond the formally assigned roles and titles, are symbols of inspiration and reassurance. The way you lead 'from the front' by personal example will create our own Organizational Ethos.

"Let's take a break and come back to discuss what kind of techniques we can use to increase our Execution Capability."

After the break, Mark dived into specific methods he wanted to implement. He started by saying, "It's important for an organization, especially one that plays the Product Innovation game, to have a systematic way of gaining and sharing knowledge. We want to practice a balanced way of achieving that." He projected a chart to the group.

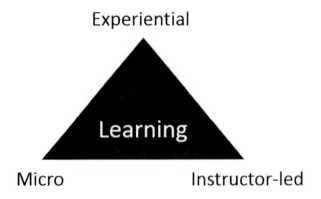

Experiential

Learning

Micro   Instructor-led

"Experiential Learning is what we discussed when we referred to using Retrospectives, to understand and improve on personal and collective experiences. Micro Learning is about using very small learning units such as short movies for skill-based understanding and learning. And Instructor-led Learning is classical classroom learning.

"Why do you need a balance of those? Because classroom learning isn't scalable or agile enough. On-boarding new employees using only classroom learning is expensive and slow. Micro learning makes the information easy to absorb but can be only a prelude to experiential and classroom learning."

"And how would you measure the progress of this balanced learning?" asked Michael.

"Glad you asked. And glad that you already think in metrics-driven management. I used the following method with great success.

"Each knowledge learning event is assigned a number of Continuous Education Credits. The number reflects the effort AND value of that particular learning event. In the case of micro learning and instructor-led learning, that's simple. For example, if you use as rule of thumb that ten minutes of time would be worth one credit, then one hour of classroom learning would be six credits. And then you adjust with value. So one hour of instructor-led Negotiations Skills training might be six credits in effort. However, the knowledge is valuable so we might assign ten credits for that course instead of six. Makes sense?" asked Mark.

But what about experiential learning?" asked Michael.

"That might be not as straight forward as the other two types, but you can still manage it. For example, I learn to use on my own a CAD/CAM software. I can go to my supervisor/coach and ask him to witness how I'm using certain features in real applications. The supervisor would have a catalog of skills that are valuable to the company. Each one would have pre-defined credits, so when you demonstrate a certain skill, you can earn the number of credits assigned to that skill."

"Oh, that's quite simple and practical," said Michael

"Correct. Pragmatism—that's what we're looking for. Starting next month, we'll introduce the new Continuous Education program where each employee will have as a personal target to earn a minimum of 50 credits a month as part of his or her Key Performance Indicators," explained Mark.

"That's a lot to absorb in one day," concluded Michael. "It's time to adjourn and prepare for dinner."

Behavioral Fit

The next morning, Mark opened the session by saying, "Yesterday morning, we covered the first quadrant (The Business Model) and in the afternoon the second quadrant (The Execution Capability). Now I want to introduce the third quadrant, which deals with the Behavioral Fit of a person to a role in the organization."

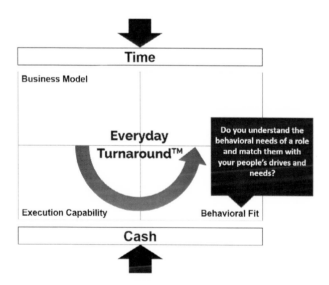

Mark continued, "By the end of this session, you should have a better understanding of the team and the people in your organization. And you'll have new tools available for you to lead effectively.

"This quadrant asks if you understand the drives and needs of the people in your organization, and if they are now in roles that enable their natural drives and needs.

"To effectively understand your people, you need to learn how your own behaviors impact your interactions with co-workers, clients, vendors, and anyone else in your day-to-day work environment. You need to understand how valuable behavioral differences are and learn to celebrate them. You also need to understand what makes your people 'tick' for we're not all the same. Different people have different drives and needs.

"You already know how hard it is to recruit the right people and, once you have them, it's hard to keep them. Finding and replacing people is a costly, time-consuming proposition. From there, you need to 'fight the war with the soldiers you have.' This means transforming what you already have into an effective workforce. Only when you've exhausted all your options *internally* do look for help *externally*.

"You already had the PI read-back session and experienced firsthand how powerful it is. How do you feel about learning how to do it?"

Robert was first to show his enthusiasm. "I thought you were kidding when you gave me the readback. I couldn't believe how much you knew about me after only five minutes. As a scientist, I became curious about how you could dissect my needs so fast and accurately predict my behavior. I wanted to ask you if I could take the course for myself. I'd definitely volunteer to pay for it."

Mark smiled and said, "No need to pay anything. I believe it's time for all of you to gain this knowledge about yourself and use it in your day-to-day activities. We'll soon be able to leverage a common language to describe behavior. That's difficult to do it in plain English and requires multiple pages for each person. Instead, we'll have a pattern diagram on one page that will speak volumes about each one of us. It also allows us to be transparent with our needs.

"I'll be the first to hang on my door the Predictive Index Placard," said Mark, showing his placard to the team.

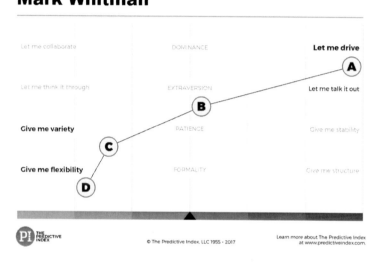

How to Interact with
Mark Whitman

"This is so cool. Can I have mine and do the same thing?" asked Michael.

"We'll have all the placards printed and laminated so you can post yours also. It will send a strong message to others that we're here to first understand them and then set them up for success. We'll have placards made for all our employees. I expect to see them visible at their workplaces," Mark suggested.

"Now, it's time to introduce Julie, our Predictive Index Trainer, who will spend the second half of the day leading the workshop Managing People to Perform. It will provide you with the insight and perspective needed to increase your self-awareness and understand what drives day-to-day behaviors. So let's get started."

After the afternoon session, the participants had gained a firm grasp of their own management and communication styles. They also could identify how best to communicate with and manage their direct reports. By the end of the workshop, the team had a behavioral team summary, a manager scorecard highlighting gaps that where inhibiting employee performance, and a detailed action plan for improving workplace communication and productivity.

The second morning of the two-day off-site, Mark opened with a "lessons learned" review of the previous day and then said, "It's time to complete the Behavioral Fit process as a team assignment. We'll practice how to create a behavioral description for a role."

In his PI toolbox, Mark had the PI Job Assessment. It was a short questionnaire that generated a behavioral pattern report for a position that could be directly compared with an individual's pattern. The questionnaire allowed each team member to describe what he/she thought were the behavioral needs of a particular job. This generated a graphic pattern that could be compared with the patterns from other team members and used to debate a job's behavioral needs. It articulated each member's opinions across the four primary factors of behavior: dominance, extroversion, patience, and formality.[25]

"Can somebody suggest a role that would be interesting to describe?" asked Mark.

"We heard a lot about the Scrum Master role that's new to us. Can we try that?" asked Robert.

---

[25]   Dominance, Extraversion, Patience, and Formality. See Appendix.

"OK, Scrum Master it is," Mark responded. As you Robert, and Michael are going to interact with this person on a day to day basis, you should provide input for the role description. "In the next three minutes, both of you will receive a link to a Job Assessment Survey that describes the Scrum Master job. Please complete the survey. Once you're done, I'll show you what each one of you thought of the Scrum Master role, and we'll use these opinions to negotiate a final behavioral description."

Once both completed the survey, Mark showed these results:

SCRUM Master Job Assesment
Completed by

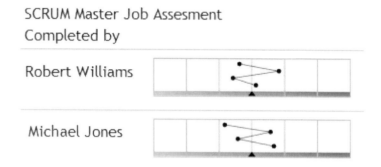

Robert Williams

Michael Jones

"As you can see from the patterns you described, you're not far apart from each other. Both of you expressed that the focus of this position is working with and through others, building and maintaining relationships, and operating closely and accurately within established guidelines. Both of you showed the need for an effective communicator, someone who can motivate others while being aware of and responsive to their needs and concerns.

"Although the results fell mostly into these two categories, and they both look very close, I see nuances that can make a lot of difference. For example, do you need a formal, social, and proper person who likes to collaborate but prefers to work together rather than delegating details? Or is it a person who can delegate details using a strong, friendly follow-up style?"

Robert replied, "As I understood the role from the Scrum training, we're looking for a person who needs to be strong and friendly on follow up. It's like being a 'friendly' sergeant in the army."

"I see what you are saying, Robert," commented Michael. "That makes sense."

SCRUM Master

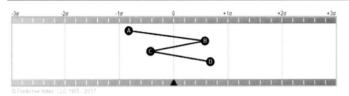

After making the adjustments, Mark printed this Job Assessment Report.

The focus of this position is working with and through others, building and maintaining relationships, and working closely and accurately within established guidelines.

There is a need for an effective communicator, someone who can stimulate and motivate others while being aware of and responsive to their needs and concerns. There will be many different people to work with. The person in this position must be friendly and genuinely interested in the business, agenda, and needs of others, including the company, its management, the team, the company's customers, or all of the above.

A persuasive, teaching style is required to communicate the company's policies, programs, and systems. A faster-than-average pace will be the norm for this position.

Detail work is a major focus of the job, and those details need to be handled quickly, correctly, and efficiently. This portion of the work focuses on relationships with others; correctly handling the details dealing with others is necessary to maintain and grow relationships.

If the job involves managing others, following up carefully, closely, and cheerfully is required. This ensures both accuracy of the work and nurturing of the relationships. Necessary corrections must be made in a constructive, supportive manner.

As time is usually a factor, the work must be done quickly as well as correctly. In general, it's important to follow guidelines, structure, and established policies closely while working with and for others.

After hearing this, Michael said, "This is remarkably accurate to what I had in mind but couldn't articulate."

Mark replied, "Of course, this is the purpose of the exercise. It provides a language to describe a role from a behavioral point of view so you can match candidates to it."

"It's what we would call check for Behavioral Fit."

Organizational Design

When Mark joined Energon, he was asked to sign the acknowledgment of a long Employee Handbook. Out of curiosity, Mark browsed the document to understand how big of a red tape to expect going forward.

One week in the job, he asked if any written policies existed. He was told the company had a well-organized set of policies called Standard Operating Procedures or SOPs. These were long documents looking freakishly complicated and stored on a server few people had access to. These documents had a lot of detail. No one knew how some of the policies had come about.

So Mark started the last session of the off-site by challenging the effectiveness of these SOPs.

"Let's talk about Standard Operating Procedures. I took the time to go through some of the SOPs and basically got lost in them after five pages. So, my question is, how useful do you think they are in their present form, and how many of them are actually used in our day-to-day activities?"

Michael went defensive. "These SOPs are important because they precisely describe what needs to be done."

Mark countered, "I'm not arguing that the information contained in them isn't useful. I'm just saying it's difficult to digest and is hardly precise enough when describing the required operations and the resulting information."

"So how would you do it differently then?" asked Michael.

"I had the privilege to run two turnarounds in the software industry. That's when I learned Scrum. But I also noticed they were using a specific language to capture the business artifacts of a business process they were trying to automate with their software. And it wasn't a written language; it was a graphical language called Universal Modelling Language or UML. It consists of different types of diagrams that will, together, help you describe the boundary of a system, the structure of a system, and the behavior of a system.

"Let me give you an example. I took an SOP—the one talking about how we open new projects that's twenty pages long. Let me show you how twenty pages of words can be condensed into two UML diagrams: a Use Case and a Class Diagram.

"The Use Case diagram shows the actors in the process and the activities that they perform in a certain sequence." Mark projected the Use Case diagram.

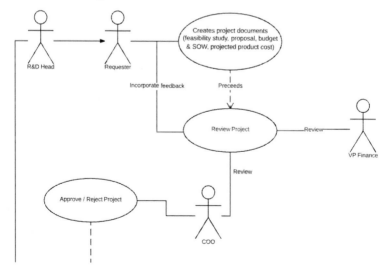

"The Class Diagram shows the objects that are managed by the process with attributes, operations, and relationships among objects." Then he showed the Class Diagram to the group.

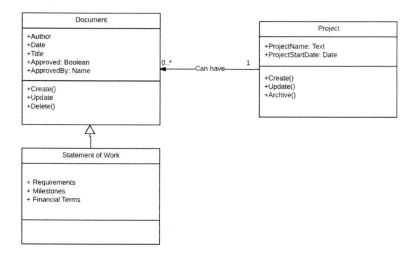

Impressed with how simple but in the same time information rich where these diagrams, Michael said, "It's remarkable how these diagrams capture the essence and the detail of the process."

Mark explained, "I can't stress enough the fact that a good, easy-to-understand description of a process, including what information is carried and processed by that process, is essential to effectively using this knowledge in day-to-day activities. Not only it needs to be clear but it has to be in a format and amount of detail that allow information technology to support the process."

He continued, "Now, you can probably anticipate that the last step in the Everyday Turnaround is Organizational Design. That's the collection of processes and roles an organization employs to achieve its strategic objectives."

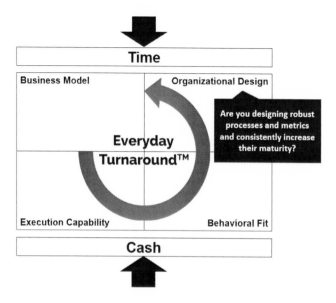

"The key to a good organizational design is clarity of process and metrics that would allow the business to continuously improve its operations. How well are these operations are managed can be measured using a scale called the Capability Maturity Model (CMM)."[26]

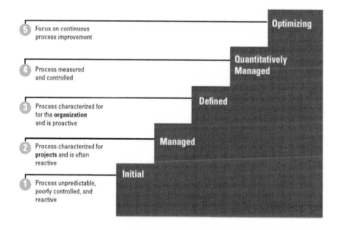

---

[26]   Capability Maturity Model (CMM) broadly refers to a process improvement approach developed by the Carnegie-Mellon Software Engineering Institute for the US Air Force.

"The scale helps describe a process maturity in a very useful way.

At the Initial Level (Level 1) a process is unpredictable, poorly controlled, and reactive. I call this the heroic level. Success in these situations depends on the competence and heroics of the people in the organization and not on the use of proven processes. This means that you are in danger of having your people burn out and become "irreplaceable".

At the Managed Level (Level 2) you see that work is organized in projects that have clear requirements and you report progress on achievement of these requirements.

At the Defined Level (Level 3) you standardize processes. Instead of re-inventing the wheel for each project like in Level 2, you pro-actively build a library of standard processes and adapt them to the job at hand within permitted guidelines. This provides consistency across the organization resulting in an ability to predict process quality, or in other words you have a clearly identified a pattern that could produce the expected result.

At the Quantitively Managed Level (Level 4), you define specific goals for a process and measure against them. You usually use statistical and other quantitative techniques. At Level 4 processes become quantitively predictable, or in other words you should consistently get the same results over time.

Finally, at the Optimizing Level (Level 5), you focus on continuous improvement of the process because of the quantitative understanding of the common causes of variations inherent in processes"

With that explanation, the team spent the rest of the session experimenting with UML on some of the company's most critical processes and evaluating the maturity level of each process.

Execute

Open Book

Mark knew that individual and team engagement in productivity and detailed cost management was crucial to a fast and cost-effective turnaround. There was simply no time in a day to have a select number of people analyze the numbers, assuring that an entire organization will make sound decisions fast. He had been in the middle of an ugly turnaround at the beginning of his career when an amazing book caught his attention. It was the *Great Game of Business* by Jack Stack. It told the story of a highly successful turnaround when Open Book Management as a method was first described.

The key concept of Open Book Management was that the information received by employees should not only help them do their jobs effectively but help them understand how the company is doing as a whole. Leaders would provide all relevant financial information about the company so they can make better decisions as workers.

When Mark read the book, he was at a serious impasse and could not see how he could make an organization of 3,000 people understand the mission of his job and act in alignment with that mission. He spent the night reading the entire book, being consumed by the ideas and the pragmatism of its implementation. Since then, he has made Open Book Management one of the pillars of his turnaround strategy.

Fast forward and compare today to the original experience of Jack Stack. He created this concept in 1983 when electronic spreadsheets weren't yet invented. Today, inexpensive Cloud-based tools could allow any employee to have real time access to financial information 24/7.

Yet although the technology changed, the principles remained the same:

- Know and teach the rules: Every employee should be given the measures of business success and taught to understand them.

- Follow the Action & Keep Score: Every employee should be expected and enabled to use his or her knowledge to improve performance.

- Provide a Stake in the Outcome: Every employee should have a direct stake in the company's success *and* in its risk of failure.

- The company should share finances as well as critical data with all employees.

- Employees are challenged to move the numbers in a direction that improves the company.

- Employees share in the company's prosperity.

The real measure of success of Open Book Management is when employees understand the numbers to a level that they can predict outcomes.

Mark had an aha moment on this before. He had introduced Open Book Management in one of his turnarounds and taught employees how to calculate their bonuses at the end of the quarter based on Open Book Information made available to them in real time. One day, his HR manager called and said that the spouse of a worker called them and asked for the numbers. She wanted to calculate her husband's bonus and see if they'd have enough money to buy a dishwasher.

To make Open Book Management effective, you cannot overwhelm people with information, even though it's now available quickly and in large volumes. You need to focus them on a few critical numbers. Once these metrics are identified and people are educated to understand them, then they become effective drivers of day-to-day activities.

Mark would put these critical numbers on display on large TVs across the company. These would be his "Information Radiators." In fact, he'd often challenge employees to talk to him in numbers because "without data you're just a person with an opinion" in the words of the great W. Edwards Deming.[27]

---

[27] W. Edwards. Deming is the father of continuous quality improvement., known as a critical contributor to the dramatic turnaround of post-war Japanese industry.

Scaling

With the organizational changes in place, sales started to grow fast.

Energon naturally went through a period of growing pains, expanding manufacturing rapidly to meet demand. The new product lines required new skills and more people. Recruiting and Onboarding new employees became a serious bottleneck.

In one of the Sprint Retrospectives, Michael raised the issue of speeding up the process. He said, "It's taking us a long time to absorb new employees. Mark, do you have any ideas on how can we can speed up the process and not compromise on quality?"

"Sure, I have a couple of tested ideas. I faced fast growth many times, and I was able to reduce onboarding times by an average of 60%," answered Mark.

"One thing that worked well was having all new employees go through on line training BEFORE they show up for their first day of work. We prepared short movies covering company mission and culture, a message from the CEO, basic rituals and what to expect in the first 30 days. That meant that on the first day of work, they already had a good idea of how things were done in our business."

"I can see how that would work," said Michael, showing his enthusiasm with the idea.

Mike continued, "The second thing we did was to put the Scrum Masters in charge of Onboarding. They would prepare a detailed Onboarding schedule for the first 30 days that would fill every minute of the new employee day. Additionally, each new employee would be assigned a Coach who would be measured on the success of the Onboarding at the end of the Onboarding month."

Friction

Mark defined friction as anything that would slow down the activity of the company. And he meant ANYTHING. Even small things such as "the lock is broken in the bathroom" would be considered friction.

The key to reduce friction was to make it highly visible. He categorized friction events as Blockers, Bugs, and Late Incidents.

A Blocker would be an impediment to complete a task that was blocked by somebody else.

A Bug would be something that did not work as expected.

A Late Incident would be when people would show up late to a meeting they'd agreed to attend.

All these would be immediately recorded in the same software used to run Scrum. They'd be posted on TVs including Dashboards showing an evolution of friction per company and division. Counting the number of bugs or incidents was not enough. There was a need to prioritize. That's why each bug had a pain level associated with it.

Pain Level	Description	Expected Resolution Time
1 HURTS A LITTLE BIT	**MILD** Pain is very mild, barely noticeable. Most of the time you don't think about it.	60 - 90 days
2 HURTS A LITTLE MORE	**TOLERABLE** Annoying and may have occasional stronger twinges.	30 Days
3 HURTS EVEN MORE	**DISTRESSFUL** It can't be ignored for more than a couple of hours, but with effort you still can manage to work	10 Days
4 HURTS A WHOLE LOT	**SEVERE** Activity is severely limited	3 Days
5 HURTS WORST	**DISABLING** <u>Must</u> take care of pain.	Today

The faster the company moved the more painful friction became. Weekly sessions of Friction retrospectives where hold by every team and employees where encouraged and given support to address them in pragmatic ways.

There was also a special type of friction. It hadn't happened yet, but there were signs it *will* happen. An example would be the soldering equipment shows signs of wear and tear and will soon need maintenance.

It's Not Over Until It's Over

All is Lost

The news that ACME Inc. canceled its orders and moved to another supplier went like a shock wave throughout the organization. ACME represented 20% of the top-line revenue and was considered a flagship customer.

When the news reached the board, the chairman felt compelled to call an emergency board meeting to discuss the situation.

Next morning, Mark woke up with a knot in his stomach. He was about to face the board, knowing the discussion could go either way. Losing ACME was what Jerry predicted before he was fired. The only way Mark could argue his position was by communicating facts. He had put together a presentation of his short-term turnaround plan and took it to the meeting.

All the board members showed concern on their faces. James, the chairman, opened the meeting.

"Good morning, everybody. I called this meeting to discuss the last two months that culminated with the loss of ACME as a client. The board is concerned that the situation is getting out of control. Mark, we need to understand the reasons for your decisions."

"Good morning. Thank you for calling this meeting. I already intended to ask you for one," replied Mark.

"Yes," he continued, "ACME notified us about switching to another supplier. This might look like a huge problem, taking into account that ACME represented 20% of our annual revenue. Mr. Chairman, remember I had told you the situation would get worse before it gets better. ACME is one of these 'get worse' moments. But I'd like to demonstrate that this was expected and is actually a blessing in disguise."

"How so?" asked James.

"ACME represents 20% of our revenue but only 3% of our gross margin contribution. All the products sold to ACME were commodity products, and we have three competitors constantly underbidding us for this account. Moreover, the products are at the end of their reasonable lifetime. The production line for them is old and needs constant repairs."

"So how do you plan to recover from the loss of ACME?" asked one of the board members.

"The plan for an economic turnaround is presented on this slide. As you can see, the first order of battle is to increase the overall contribution margin of our products but at the same time kill any product with margins that contribute below 20%."

"But how will you then cover your fixed costs?" another board member asked.

"The plan is to have all our fixed costs paid by the high-volume low-margin products and make our profits from the low-volume high-margin products. We should end up with 80% of our gross margin coming from high-end applications. With the fixed costs paid by the low-margin products, sales on high-margin products will go directly to our bottom line."

"And how will you create this high-margin product line?" asked James.

"Well, our second order of battle is to switch from 'cost-plus pricing' to 'value-based pricing' and stop leaving money on the table. This company has over engineered products for the markets it's pursuing. But it's not using this advantage to move into high-margin applications because it seems they'll yield a low volume. For the products that are currently in less price-sensitive applications, we intend to raise prices 30% on average. Then we plan to go after extreme conditions applications with margins above 50% where we have practically no competition."

"And you think this approach will turn the tide?"

"This plan combined with a 50% reduction in overhead should swing us from a ten-million-dollar annual loss to a positive seven million in the next twelve months."

Mark had just shifted the conversation from emotions and opinions to facts. Those around the table seemed to grasp the situation logically.

"OK. So how fast can you show us results?" asked James. With that question, Mark knew he's just gained the time he needed.

Turnaround

Over the course of the next 12 months, Energon developed a couple of products for the Thermal Interfaces[28] market and built a completely new sales channel for this market. These products were extremely well received, and the new division started to generate substantial cash flow. This provided the company with a second leg to stand on.

Growth was exponential and 24 months from the start of the turnaround, both divisions were racing each other in revenue growth—a sign the company was firmly aligned and executing well on a rising tide for both markets.

Mark came to work every day and watched how the company was effectively operating without too much employee handholding. The culture of rowing in the same direction was now so strong, he could have taken vacation for a month and no one would have noticed.

Mark suggested it's time to prepare for an IPO—an idea that met with a lot of enthusiasm. The next step was to hire an investment banker and file for an IPO.

---

[28] A material that has very high thermal conductivity and is used to transfer heat from an electronic device like a microprocessor to a heatsink

"Der mentsh trakht un Got lakht.[29] Man plans and God laughs." Mark remembered this old Jewish proverb his mother used to tell him when he'd become invested in his own plans. It took him a long time in his career to learn to let go and let life unfold.

Two weeks before the IPO, Energon received three offers to be acquired. In subsequent counter bidding, the price reached $300m, a 15 times increase in value since Mark took over. For Mark, it was time to let go . . .

---

[29]   Jewish proverb in Yiddish

The Tools

Everyday Turnaround Framework

The Everyday Turnaround tactical framework is an approach to transform existing organizations. It contrasts with the way you would setup a new organization.

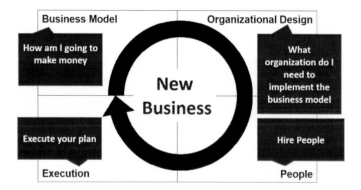

In a **new** business, you would first think of a business model that can make you money. Then you would design an organization (roles and processes) that would be able to operate your business model. Then you would hire people and execute your plan.

With an **existing** business, you are faced with 2 critical constrains. Time and Cash

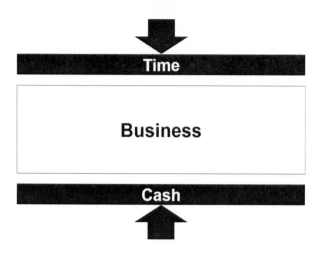

These constrains are severely limiting your options. You need to go through the same steps but in reverse order, using a different approach based on agile tactics to shorten the cycle.

The first step is the Business Model. You need to check if with the existing products or knowledge you can reach fast product market fit.

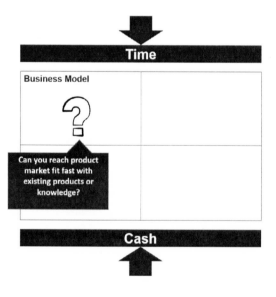

If you cannot, then your chances to recover are very slim because investor patience is very limited in distressed situations. No time to invent new things, just enough time to repurpose what you have and execute flawlessly.

The second step is Execution Capability. You need to build that fast and most importantly, you need to do it with the people and resources available at that time.

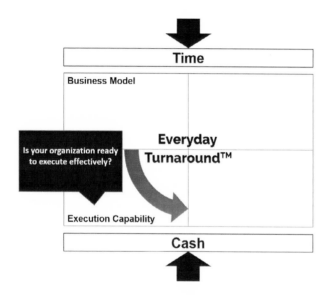

In other words, you need to fight the battle with the soldiers you have, not with the soldiers you would like to have.

The third step is Behavioral Fit. You need to understand the behavioral needs of the existing roles and see if they match your people's natural drives and needs, or in other words match the behavioral patterns of the roles with those ot the person's occupying that role.

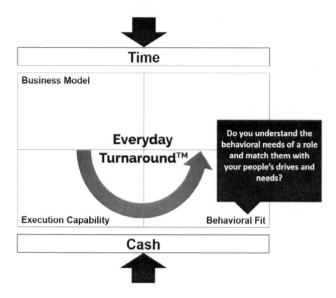

This would dramatically reduce the stress a role creates if a person is aligned to the behavioral requirements of the role, thus requiring less energy to adapt.

The fourth step is Organizational Design.

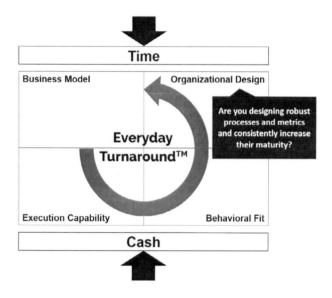

In this step, you are systematically redesigning your processes and implementing the right metrics and systems to manage them.

This cycle repeats by checking periodically your assumptions about your business model

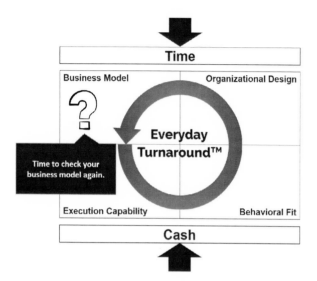

The Predictive Index™

The Behavioral Assessment

The Predictive Index[30] set of behavioral and cognitive assessment tools was started by Arnold Daniels in the early 1950. The original tool, called the *Predictive Index Behavioral Assessment™*, was developed to objectify workplace behaviors so you can predict the drives and motivations of others, be a better manager, and communicate more effectively. It's a highly effective, yet simple, scientifically validated assessment that measures four core behavioral drives. Where these drives fall creates a behavioral pattern that provides a simple framework for understanding the workplace behaviors of your people.

Following this was the Predictive Index Job Assessment, designed to capture the behavioral and cognitive requirements of a specific role while considering company culture and team dynamics.

Arnold Daniels developed his assessment through a normative sample of thousands of people. Data collected from this sample was used to identify a normal range of behavioral factor levels for the adult working population (e.g., what is high, average, and low).

---

[30] The Predictive Index is a trademark and tools owned by the Predictive Index. Any reference to Predictive Index is used with permission from The Predictive Index Inc.

Typically, benchmarked samples only allow you to see how someone falls on a spectrum relative to others in the working population.

While the PI Behavioral Assessment leverages this benchmarking methodology, it reaches beyond typical people-to-people differences to provide a lens into distinct drives and needs by comparing behavioral factors.

For example, even though two people may have equal levels of dominance as compared to each other, one person may have a high level of extraversion relative to his/her level of dominance while the other is low in comparison. The relational difference between each person's dominance level and extraversion level represents a highly different set of drives and needs. These differences impact how people function at their best in the workplace.

The Learning Indicator

The last addition to the toolset is the Predictive Index Learning Indicator™, a cognitive ability assessment that measures an individual's capacity to learn, adapt, and grasp new concepts in the workplace.

Think of it this way: Picture your brain as a sponge with you IQ being the size of the sponge. What cognitive dimension measures is not the *size* of the sponge but, how *fast* the sponge will absorb new things. This way, you can scientifically tell how fast someone will learn a new job and how that person will behave in this new environment.

Nearly a century of research has been devoted to understanding and measuring cognitive abilities. General cognitive ability can be roughly defined as "the ability to understand complex ideas, to adapt effectively to the environment, to learn from experience, to engage in various forms of reasoning, and to overcome obstacles by taking thought." (Neisser, 1996)

There is near-unanimous agreement that a single underlying factor of cognitive abilities exists: the "g" factor. This is important because it means a measurement of "g" correlates to measurements of more-specific forms of cognitive abilities, like fluid intelligence (reasoning skills), crystallized intelligence (language, reading, and spelling), memory, visual perception, auditory perception, retrieval (creativity and fluency), and speed (reaction time and perceptual speed).

Since the measurement of "g" as provided by the PI Learning Indicator is a strong indicator of how a person is likely to perform on more specific ability tests, it indicates how well they will handle job-related cognitive tasks.

Line of Sight™

Line-of-Sight™ is a nine-minute diagnostic where employees respond to 29 questions. It was developed by Prana Business Consulting.

The Survey revealed gaps in alignment across what the method calls the Keys to Strategy Execution™. These would be Strategic Understanding, Leadership, Balanced Metrics, Activities and Structure, Human Capital and Market Discipline. It would reveal if the Key was aligned, misaligned, somewhat aligned or not sure of alignment. It is using the Confidence-Based Marking to determine the level of alignment across the Keys of Strategy Execution

Line-Of-Sight is a trademark Prana Business Consulting. Any reference to Line-Of-Sight is used with permission Prana Business Consulting

Scrum

The name Scrum comes from a paper written by two Japanese management thinkers, Akeuchi and Nonaka, about a new way to develop new products. The term Scrum refers to the game of rugby to stress the importance of teams.

In rugby, "scrum" refers to an ordered formation of players used to restart play. The forwards of a team form up with arms interlocked and heads down, and they push forward against a similar group from the opposing side. The ball is thrown into the scrum, and the players try to gain possession of it by kicking it backward toward their own side.

Akeuch and Nanaka used the analogy between a team sport like rugby and being successful at new product development. Their conclusion was that the best teams are those that are given direction within which they have room to devise their own tactics on how to best head toward their joint objective and require autonomy to achieve excellence.

Scrum in business refers to an agile framework for completing complex projects. It was originally formalized for software development projects, but it works well for any complex, innovative scope of work.

This is the Scrum framework in 30 seconds as described by the SCRUM Alliance[31]:

- A product owner creates a prioritized wish list called a product backlog.

- During sprint planning, the team pulls a small chunk from the top of that wish list, a sprint backlog, and decides how to implement those pieces.

- The team has a certain amount of time—a sprint (usually two to four weeks)—to complete its work, but it meets each day to assess its progress (daily Scrum).

- Along the way, the Scrum Master keeps the team focused on its goal.

- At the end of the sprint, the work should be potentially shippable—that is, ready to hand to a customer, put on a store shelf, or show to a stakeholder.

- The sprint ends with a sprint review and retrospective.

- As the next sprint begins, the team chooses another chunk of the product backlog and begins working again.

---

[31]   www.scrumalliance.org

UML

The **Unified Modeling Language (UML)** is a general-purpose Modeling Language in the field of <u>software engineering</u>, that is intended to provide a standard way to visualize the design of a system.

UML consists of many types of Diagrams but the most used ones for business purposes are the Use Case, Class, State Machine and Activity Diagram.

In 1997 UML was adopted as a standard by the Object Management Group (OMG), and has been managed by this organization ever since. In 2005 UML was also published by the International Organization for Standardization (ISO) as an approved ISO standard.

The OODA loop

Focusing on how well time is managed will create a shorter decision-making cycle giving an extraordinary competitive advantage to a business. It's based on a concept by John Boyd, a brilliant military strategist in the United States Air Force. He called it the OODA Loop.

According to Boyd, decision-making occurs in a recurring cycle of observe-orient-decide-act. An organization that can process this cycle quickly, observing and reacting to unfolding events more rapidly than an opponent can thereby "get inside" the opponent's decision cycle and gain the advantage.

Orientation (The second O)—is the most important part of the O-O-D-A loop since it shapes the way we observe, the way we decide, the way we act. It is strongly influenced by the company culture and previous experiences.

The OODA Loop shows that prior to making a decision (the Decide phase), the person will first have to get information (Observe) and determine what it means to him and what he can do about it (Orient).

The OODA loop, which focuses on strategic military requirements, was adapted for business in the form of PDCA (plan-do-check-act, sometimes seen as plan-do-check-adjust). It is a repetitive four-stage model for continuous improvement (CI) in business process management. The PDCA model is also known as the Deming circle/cycle/wheel. PDCA was popularized by Dr. W. Edwards Deming, an American engineer, statistician, and management consultant. Deming is often considered the father of modern quality control.

PI Reports

Mark's Predictive Index Results

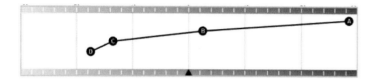

Strongest Behaviors: Mark's PI Pattern is extremely wide, which means his behaviors are very strongly expressed and his needs are very strongly felt.

Mark expresses the following behaviors:

Strongly venturesome in taking risks and focusing on the future: He's almost exclusively concerned with where he's going rather than either how he'll get there or where he's been. Very adaptable: He solves problems as they occur rather than through planning.

Makes decisions and takes action, even when there's an absence of proof confirming his decision. Comfortable operating outside of traditions, he pursues strongly innovative ideas, even in the face of failures or popular opposition.

Remarkably independent: He resists authority and proven "by the book" methods in favor of his own ideas.

Intense proactivity and aggressiveness in driving to reach his goals: He actively and boldly challenges the world, his business, and even others' areas within his business.

Strongly independent in putting forth his own ideas: They are innovative and original and, if implemented, will change the organization. Resourceful and forceful in overcoming obstacles, he vigorously and directly attacks problems, and he fights back hard when challenged.

Incredibly strong sense of urgency: He's in nearly constant motion, putting pressure on himself and others for immediate results. He's unable to do routine work.

Summary

Mark is a very independent, confident, decisive, self-starter, intense and driving. He has a strong sense of urgency, can react and adjust quickly to changing conditions. He can generate novel ideas and deal with them swiftly.

His drive is directed at getting done what he believes need to be done. Competitive, ambitious, and venturesome, he responds positively and actively to challenge and pressure, always sure of his ability to handle problems and people.

Mark is an outgoing and poised person, a forceful, animated, communicator tending to be more authoritative than persuasive in his style. He talks briskly with assurance and conviction, and is a stimulating influence on others, while being direct, determined, and flexible in dealing with them.

Sure of the value of his own judgments and opinions, he's persistent in defending them if put under pressure to change them. He will question and challenge established company policies or systems and strive to prove in action the value of his own ideas for change.

More concerned with achieving goals than the details of how things get done, Mark freely delegates to others with loose follow-up, but with demand and pressure for timely results. Ingenious and venturesome, he will become restless and dissatisfied if required to work under close control or to do work that's routine or highly structured. Very much a generalist, Mark is more concerned with the strategies involved in reaching his goals than with specific or detailed tactics.

Management Style

As a manager of people or projects, Mark will be:

Broadly focused, fast moving, and aggressive in pursuit of his own goals

Eager to delegate details and implementation plans, leaving him to focus on new ideas

Reluctant to delegate true authority. He will eagerly discuss ideas with others and enjoys that process; however, his inner conviction is often too strong to convince him to change his mind.

His follow-up is quick and cursory. Mark is likely to consider details minutia or impediments to focusing on the bigger picture.

Constantly looking to improve performance and ability to compete, he's willing to try radically new solutions and innovative approaches.

An influential and stimulating team leader, he encourages others to look at things from entirely new perspectives. He's relentless in his pursuit of change and creativity.

Direct, spontaneous, and opinionated, he's quick to voice his opinion of how things are going.

Influencing Style

As an influencer, Mark will be:

Authoritative and enthusiastic in driving the process toward the goal—a "no-holds-barred" approach. Motivated to keep the process moving as quickly as possible, he's comfortable thinking on his feet and spontaneously removing barriers to success while focused on the result.

Willing to take risks, he's unabashedly enthusiastic about unconventional or innovative methods to solve problems and gain agreements.

He's better at influencing others about intangibles such as ideas or concepts than highly specialized or detail-oriented tangibles.

Strong at gaining agreements, he's comfortable taking the risks associated with asking for the decision after only general discussions of the problem and how to solve it. He's not focused on implementation details.

Driven, competitive, and independent, he prefers to make decisions with unrestricted leeway and authority.

Management Strategies

To maximize his effectiveness, productivity, and job satisfaction, consider providing Mark with the following:

High levels of autonomy and flexibility in his job

Ample opportunity for expression of and action on his own ideas and initiatives

Variety, challenge, responsibility, and opportunities to prove himself

Recognition, advancement, and tangible rewards for success

John's Predictive Index Results

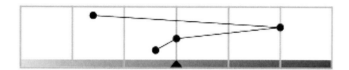

John is a friendly, congenial, and outgoing person who can get along well with just about anybody. He meets people easily and enjoys doing so. He feels just as comfortable in group activities as he is one on one.

He can connect with others while being aware of, and responsive to, their needs and interests. An unselfish person, he derives satisfaction from doing things for other people. He's most comfortable when he feels accepted by others and respected for his helpful nature. Patient and understanding, he is a particularly good listener. People find him easy to talk to and feel little pressure from this easy-going individual.

His unselfish and uncritical interest in others is helpful in developing and maintaining personal relationships. So is his ability to recognize and accommodate widely differing points of view. He "wears well" in repeated contacts, and will generally put the interests of others, including company management, customers, or his team members, first. John is an open communicator of ideas, programs, or decisions, and readily accepts the ideas or decisions of others.

When he faces risk in his decisions, he will work closely with others—his team, trusted advisors, management, or subject matter experts—to ensure inclusion and representation of their interests. The same holds true when he needs to deviate from agreed-upon processes.

Informal in style, John is casual about strictly adhering to company policy or the precise accuracy of the details of his work, preferring to delegate details to others. Working steadily at an unhurried pace, he has the kind of patience required to do consistent and/or repetitive work over long periods. It's work that, in this case, should involve considerable contact with people.

John is a stable person who functions best working in a familiar environment among familiar people and would be less effective if required to work in frequently changing, highly technical, or very detail-oriented positions. This modest person has high levels of team orientation and collaboration; his understanding of others and ability to get along well with them are strong qualities.

As a manager of people or projects, John will be:

- Interested in maintaining a loyal, stable, established team that delivers consistent, reliable results for the company

- Unselfishly interested in working with and through others; he's a willing team member and participant, even of teams he manages.

- Especially trusting of others and inclined to delegate freely to them, his follow-up is casual and cursory. He uses subtle persuasion and trust rather than intense task-checking to ensure the work gets done.

- Respectful of authority and established processes, he will defer to established processes for guidance and seek direction from trusted advisors, his team's expertise, or management leadership in situations of risk or uncertainty.

- Conscious of change in the work environment, he will strive to maintain a consistent, stable working environment for his team with as much freedom from time pressures as possible.

- Inclusive and collaborative, John is an empathetic listener, a patient coach, and a lenient and understanding manager.

To maximize his effectiveness, productivity, and job satisfaction, consider providing John with the following:

- Opportunities for frequent contact and communication with others, particularly in a helpful role

- Individual and group recognition, especially for teams and the relationships he's built

- Excellent coaches, mentors, or trusted advisors

- A stable work environment and team

- Flexibility in how he approaches his work

- Thorough training in each job assignment with ample time for practice

Jerry's Predictive Index Results

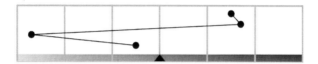

Jerry's Predictive Index pattern is extremely wide, which means his behaviors are very strongly expressed and his needs are very strongly felt.

Jerry is an engaging communicator, poised and capable of projecting enthusiasm and warmth, and of motivating other people. He has a strong sense of urgency, initiative, and competitive drive to get things done, with emphasis on working with and through people in the process. He understands people well and uses that understanding effectively in influencing others to act.

Impatient for results and particularly impatient with details and routines, Jerry is a confident and venturesome "doer" and decision-maker who will delegate details and can also delegate responsibility and authority when necessary. Jerry is a self-starter who can be skillful at training and developing others. He applies pressure for results but, in doing so, his style is more "selling" than "telling."

At ease and self-assured with groups or when making new contacts, Jerry is gregarious and extraverted. He has an invigorating impact on people and is always selling in a general sense. He learns and reacts quickly and works at a faster-than-average pace. Able to adapt quickly to change and variety in his work, he will become impatient and less effective if required to work primarily with repetitive routines and details.

In general terms, Jerry is an ambitious and driving person who is motivated by opportunity for advancement to levels of responsibility where he can use his skills as team builder, motivator, and mover.

As a salesperson, Jerry will be:

- Confident and persuasive in guiding the process toward his goal

- Eager to keep the process moving as quickly as possible: He uses persuasion, not pressure, to close a deal.

- Skillful with the emotional aspects of the sale: He connects with his prospects more than the specific details of the implementation, leveraging this information to close the deal quickly.

- Adept at navigating the politics of an organization: He finds the key players and uses persuasive talk to win the sale.

- Flexible and adaptable: He relies on his ability to think on his feet rather than make a distinct plan to follow.

- He's better at selling intangibles such as ideas or concepts than technical or specialized products.

To maximize his effectiveness, productivity, and job satisfaction, consider providing Jerry with the following:

- Opportunities for involvement and interaction with people
- Some independence and flexibility in his activities
- Freedom from repetitive routine and details in work, providing variety and change of pace
- Opportunities to learn and advance at a fairly fast pace
- Recognition and reward for communications and leadership skills demonstrated
- Social and status recognition as rewards for achievement

Robert's Predictive Index Results

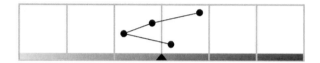

Robert is an intense, results-oriented, self-starter whose drive and sense of urgency are tempered and disciplined by his concern for the accuracy and quality of his work. His approach to anything he does or is responsible for is carefully thought out, based on thorough analysis and detailed knowledge of pertinent facts. Strongly technically oriented, he has confidence in his professional knowledge and ability to get things done quickly and correctly. With experience, he will develop a high level of expertise in his work and be highly aware of mistakes made either by himself or anyone doing work under his supervision. Robert takes his work and responsibilities very seriously and expects others to do the same.

In social matters, Robert is reserved and private, with little interest in small talk. His interest and his energy will focus primarily on his work and, in general, he is more comfortable and open in the work environment than he is in purely social situations. In expressing himself in his work environment, he is factual, direct, and authoritative.

Imaginative and venturesome, Robert is a creative person, capable of developing new ideas, systems, plans, or technology, or capable of analyzing and improving old ones. To get things done, he relies primarily on his own knowledge and thinking, with little reference to others. He sets a high, exacting standard for himself, and he generally finds that others do not meet that standard. To earn his trust, someone must consistently meet that standard and get results. If they can do that, Robert will do whatever he can to work with them whenever he needs to collaborate. While he may be perceived by others as aloof, he will earn their respect for his knowledge of his work and the soundness of his decisions.

As a manager of people or projects, Robert will be:

- Both broadly focused and tactically cognizant: Strategic thinking is a priority moderated by a drive for details, accuracy, and correctness.

- Self-reliant and independent with a great deal of confidence in his ideas, opinions, and knowledge: He has definite opinions about how things should be done and prefers at least some hands-on knowledge of what he manages.

- Hesitant to delegate authority or details: His follow-up is close and critical, ensuring that his team has completed all work to his exacting standards.

- Fast-paced and eager for results, tempered by a drive to ensure accuracy and completeness: He interprets deadlines literally and drives his team hard to meet them.

- Slow to trust others until they have produced accurate, timely results consistently: He's demanding, creative, and exacting. Always striving to do things better, faster, and with greater precision, Robert focuses more on solving problems than celebrating or praising solutions.

As an influencer, Robert will be:

- Authoritative and assertive in influencing others toward his goal

- Driven to influence others as quickly as possible without sacrificing quality in any way

- Eager to completely understand any idea or concept before bringing it before others

- Competitive and individualistic in his approach: He prefers to work alone and maintain control of the process.

- Diagnostic in approach: He asks probing questions, ascertains the problem, and applies a solution proven to work.

- He's more comfortable answering questions or objections if he's had time to think about his response and can provide proof to support it.

To maximize his effectiveness, productivity, and job satisfaction, consider providing Robert with the following:

- Opportunities to broaden the technical knowledge of his work with learning experiences in increasingly responsible positions

- As much autonomy as possible in setting priorities, expressing his ideas, and putting them into action

- Recognition for tangible results obtained, rather than for political or selling skills

- Freedom from repetition

- Technical challenges to which he can apply innovative solutions

Michael's Predictive Index Results

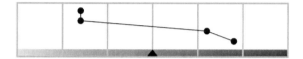

Michael is a thoughtful, disciplined person who is particularly attentive to, careful of, and accurate with the details involved in his job. He identifies problems and enjoys solving them, particularly within his area of expertise. He works at a steady, even pace, leveraging his background for the betterment of the team, company, or customer.

With experience and/or training, Michael will develop a high level of specialized expertise. He is serious and dedicated to his job and the company. His work pace is steady and even-keeled, and he's motivated by a real concern for getting work done thoroughly and correctly. His discipline and circumspect thinking will lend caution to his decision-making.

He plans ahead, double checks, and follows up carefully on his decisions and actions. A modest and unassuming person, Michael works autonomously in his area of expertise. When working outside of his expertise, his drive is to seek specialized knowledge by finding definitive answers from written resources, authoritative management, or established subject-matter experts.

He's most effective and productive when he works within or close to his own specialty and experience, and he prefers to stick to the proven way. If it becomes necessary for him to initiate or adopt change, he will need to see cold, hard, evidence to prove that the new way is proven, complete, and yields high-quality results.

In addition, Michael will carefully plan the implementation to minimize problems and maximize results. Michael is reserved and accommodating, expressing himself sincerely and factually. In general, he is rather cautious and conservative in his style, skeptical about anything new or unfamiliar, or any change in the traditional way of doing things. Possessing the ability to strongly concentrate on the job at hand, he's most effective when given uninterrupted blocks of time. He has better-than-average aptitude for work that is analytical or technical in nature.

As a manager of people or projects, Michael will be:

- Focused on providing his team with a sanctioned, proven template by which they will produce high quality, consistent work

- Respectful of authority and established regulations: He will evaluate change with skepticism, proceeding cautiously and adapting slowly after prudent analysis of the outcome

- Loyal and diligent in pursing the company's goals and protecting it from risk or failure

- Cautious, he delegates to those who have proven to him that they get results. His follow-up will be close, and he'll ensure that all procedures have been followed and all standards met.

- He's most comfortable managing functions where he has deep knowledge and expertise. Generally these functions will be more technical than social.

- Introspective and quiet: He will share his ideas with others after significant analysis and reflective consideration.

To maximize his effectiveness, productivity, and job satisfaction, consider providing Michael with the following:

- Opportunity to work within his area of expertise to assure high-quality, by-the-book, results

- Detailed, thorough training in his specialized work wherever necessary

- Chance to learn and practice in an orderly, stable environment

- Recognition for work well done

- Stability and predictability in both his work environment and his responsibilities

- A positive, non-threatening approach when it's necessary to correct, change, or criticize his work

Acknowledgments

This book would not have been possible without the unwavering support of my wife, Alina. Between work and travel running turn-arounds, I took too much time from family working at this book, and for her patience, encouragement and ideas I am so grateful.

Next, I thank the Predictive Index team for its support and advice ever since I was trained 20 years ago to build a successful consulting practice with my wife, a Certified Predictive Index Partner.

I want to acknowledge the support of Robert Jordan and Olivia Wolak of the Interim Executive Association—from the great turn-around assignments I was called to perform over the years to partic-ipation at the annual InterimExecs conferences.

Finally, I want to thank Joe Clark of Prana Business for the intro-duction to Line-of-Sight and the support in the chapters about align-ment of execution to strategy.

About the Author

Eric Kish is an author, speaker, and Turnaround CEO with 20 years' experience in transforming organizations at various stages of distress.

He is also a managing partner at Kish & Partners Consulting, a firm dedicated to teaching and helping clients implement the principles of Everyday Turnaround.

Eric is an active member of the Association of Interim Executives and currently runs or advises on turnarounds.

He has earned an MSc from Stanford Business School, an Advanced Certificate in Strategy and Innovation from MIT, and an MSc in Electrical Engineering from the Polytechnics of Bucharest.

Eric lives in Boulder, Colorado, with his wife Alina and their daughter Maya.

To learn more about Eric, please visit www.everydayturnaround.com